COMPLETE HANDBOOK OF
MUSIC GAMES AND ACTIVITIES
FOR EARLY CHILDHOOD

Margaret Athey
and
Gwen Hotchkiss

Parker Publishing Company, Inc.
West Nyack, New York

© 1982 by

Margaret Athey and Gwen Hotchkiss

Fifth Printing.....April 1987

Library of Congress Cataloging in Publication Data
Athey, Margaret, 1936-
    Complete handbook of music games and activities for early childhood.

    Includes index.
    1. Games with music. 2. Music—Instruction and study—Juvenile. I. Hotchkiss,
Gwen, 1935-
II. Title.
MT948.A76   372.8'7044   82-2289
ISBN 0-13-161083-X   AACR2

Printed in the United States of America

ABOUT THE AUTHORS

Margaret Athey is currently a music specialist in the public schools of Shawnee Mission, Kansas, and in this capacity, she has worked with students at all levels in music. She is a graduate of Indiana University School of Music, with an advanced degree from the University of Missouri at Kansas City. She is a member of her city's Art Commission and is active in the affairs of Kansas Music Educators Association and Music Educator's National Conference.

Gwen Hotchkiss is Supervisor of Elementary Music for the Shawnee Mission schools. A specialist in teacher evaluation and curriculum development, her teaching experience has spanned all grade levels from kindergarten through college. She earned degrees from Pittsburg State University and from the University of Missouri, with Advanced Administrative Certification from the University of Kansas. She is a member of Music Educator's National Conference.

Ms. Athey and Ms. Hotchkiss, individually and jointly, have presented numerous teacher workshops across the country and have published widely in leading music education journals. They are the coauthors of *A Galaxy of Games for the Music Class* and *A Treasury of Individualized Activities for the Music Class.*

A Word From the Authors on the Practical Value of This Book

The *Complete Handbook of Music Games and Activities for Early Childhood* is for both the music teacher and the classroom teacher of students of ages four through eight years. Musical games and activities are presented to teach music to young children—music skills, music concepts, music facts and music appreciation.

The child's world of play is based on repetition of sound, rhythm and movement. Play, developed into educational games and activities, is a natural way for students to experience a sense of achievement while engaging in an activity which develops a skill, an ability, or an attitude. Young students need to become actively involved as they learn to question and think and then apply these new skills to their personal environment.

Music, with its natural appeal to young learners, offers an exciting vehicle for motivating and reinforcing developmental skills during these early childhood years. Music has a special charm which can turn children "on" to their entire learning process. Through these games, students can master music skills easily. Music is more fun when they are participating in an irresistible game.

As educators, we are challenged to develop instruction for every student so that he may achieve his greatest potential. What greater way than through the expressive art of MUSIC?

Purpose

The purpose of this book is to provide the teacher with hundreds of ideas for games and activities to develop a musical awareness during the early childhood years. This book, as a teacher resource, will enable the teacher to go directly to a game or activity designed to teach a specific music skill or concept. A teacher may choose to introduce the new skill through an activity or merely use the same activity for fun and relaxation. A student might be in need of an activity to reinforce a certain skill, or he might want a special challenge or some extra fun.

This book includes a sequence of games and activities in categories of Rhythm, Melody, Singing, and Music Appreciation. Each category covers the gamut from easy games for reinforcement through the more difficult ones for challenges or enrichment. The materials can be used for activities for the entire classroom or for small groups, and even for individual students. An additional chapter is provided for the individual student in a Learning Center setting.

Organization

This book contains approximately 300 music games and activities designed for young students aged four through eight. Each activity is short and concise with specific application to learning a single music skill or fact.

The games begin with the most commonly used—rhythmic play responses. These Rhythmic Games in Part One develop from creative movement through patterned movement as students are required to remember and reproduce patterns. As their skills become more refined, the responses call for additional aural perception and discrimination along with the manipulation of rhythm instruments.

Part Two presents those skills that are essential to the development of listening, reading and writing melodies. Beginning with games and activities for reinforcing listening to melodies, a sequence is developed to teach skills in reading and writing melodies. Included are games for multisensory responses as a "readiness" is developed in matching, grouping and classifying musical symbols.

Games and activities in Part Three are for developing the singing voice. They range from the spoken language of chants through the competency of language in singing and self-expression. The development of the singing voice is presented in games for tone matching and solo singing. The imagination and development of individual creativity is further challenged in activities to encourage the original creation of songs.

An entire section (Part Four) is devoted to Music Appreciation, which encourages an awareness of our cultural heritage through music. Included are famous composers and great works of music literature. Another special feature of this part is activities for special events of the calendar year and our national holidays.

In Part Five you will find ideas for producing sounds and making instruments. There are games for learning about instruments of the band and orchestra in Part Six.

Part Seven provides help for the teacher in the creation of a Music Learning Center. Activities are presented for one or two students. They are complete with directions for creating puzzles, touchbook ideas and flannelgraph activities. Any of these activities may be used for reinforcement or additional challenges depending upon the musical skills of the learner.

The index lists activities by musical concept: rhythm, melody, tone color, and expression. A topical index is annotated to assist the teacher in locating the specific game or activity for her class.

Whether the teacher is an experienced professional seeking new ways to teach music, or a beginner hunting for ideas to motivate the young learner, the *Complete Handbook of Music Games and Activities for Early Childhood* will become an indispensable resource book.

Margaret Athey
and
Gwen Hotchkiss

CONTENTS

Introduction   **7**

Part One: Games for Rhythm   **13**

    Creative Movement – 15
    Environmental Fantasy Stories – 23
    Games for Reinforcing the Steady Beat – 32
    Games for Learning Patterned Steps – 38
    Singing Games – 47

Part Two: Games for Melody   **77**

    Listening to Melody – 79
    Reading Melody – 84
    Writing Melody – 89

Part Three: Games for Singing   **95**

    Chanting - 97
    Tone Matching – 101
    Solo Singing – 106
    Group Singing – 109
    Creating Songs – 112

**Part Four: Games for Learning About Famous
           Composers and Their Music**   **117**

    The Composers and Their Music – 121
    Games to Reinforce Knowledge of Literature
       and Composers – 145

Part Five: Games for Sound Exploration   **149**

    Ideas for Producing Sounds – 151
    Making Instruments – 163

Part Six: Games for Learning About Instruments   165

Learning About Instruments – 167
Developing an Ensemble for Rhythm Instruments – 178

Part Seven: Learning Centers   183

Where and When – 186
Using Them – 186
Designing Them – 187
Learning Centers for Listening to Music – 188
Learning Centers for Sound Exploration – 192
Learning Centers for Exploring Instruments – 196
Learning Centers for Singing – 200
Learning Centers for Music Writing – 203
Learning Centers for Other Activities – 207

Appendix   209

Index   213

Part One

GAMES FOR RHYTHM

Creative Movement 15
Environmental Fantasy Stories 23
Games for Reinforcing the Steady Beat 32
Games for Learning Patterned Steps 38
Singing Games 47

CREATIVE MOVEMENT

Young children need the opportunity to take advantage of their marvelous powers of imagination and fantasy; creativity must be encouraged. Incorporate body movement and free dramatic play into the imagery of magical stories and watch the children enjoy the wholesome and satisfying world of make-believe.

During creative movement children move through space in a free and sometimes impromptu manner. With a seemingly endless imagination, a child has opportunities for self-expression and exploration that become self-motivating challenges. The natural curiosity he brings is his greatest resource.

Teach the children to move when they hear the piano, drum, or other music; teach them to stop movement when the music stops. For a special touch of drama and satisfaction, be sure that all children learn to "freeze" at the end of each piece.

Jumping Jack

Ages:　4-6
Equipment:　Piano or recording of appropriate music
Directions:

The students recite the verse below as they dramatize the words. An additional part may be added by using music (try octave skips at the piano) while the students do jumping-jacks. When the music stops, they return to the inside of their pretend box.

Verse:

My Jack-in-the box
Snuggles down tight,
And hides very quiet

15

Way out of my sight.
Then all of a sudden,
He jumps way up high
And shows me his smile as he bobs
A "goodbye."

The Tight-Rope Walker

Ages: 4-6
Equipment: None
Directions:

As the verse is recited, the students respond with appropriate actions.

Verse:

I can walk on a tight rope in a small straight
   line and balance really quite well . . .
   And be very, very careful.
I can turn around when I get to the end
   and go back to where I started . . .
   And be very, very careful.
I can walk sideways and go step-over-step
   And never lose my balance . . .
   And be very, very careful.
I can stop in the middle and take a big bow . . .
   And be very, very careful.

My Marionette

Ages: 4-6
Equipment: None
Directions:

In this group activity, students listen to the verse and move appropriately. When they become familiar with the words, they can begin to repeat them with the teacher.

Verse:

My Marionette is a comical man,
   as he jerks, and he bobs and he nods
His arms and his head and his feet and his
   legs
As his master pulls strings and small rods.

Sometimes he is quiet with never a sound
   and suddenly he moves very quick!

He now is a soldier quite tall and straight
   with both arms and legs very stiff,
Awaiting a parade to come down the street
   so that now he can march with the band
And carry a flag, wave at people that watch,
Now isn't that really quite grand?

After marching along with kicks very high
   and arms and head, oh, so straight,
He begins to get tired and starts slowing down
   a little at first and then WAIT!
His head has gone over; his arms are all limp;
   his legs are collapsing, I fear.
He's now in a heap and his strings crumpled down;
The parade is all over this year.

Rock and Roll-Over

Ages: 4-6
Equipment: Recording of rock music
Directions:

Each player chooses a space. As the lively music begins, the player dances freely to the music. When the music stops, the player lies down on the floor and "freezes." When the music begins again, he should "roll over" and begin dancing again.

The activity level of the group can be controlled by the time spent either moving or resting.

Fluttering Scarves

Ages: 4-6
Equipment: Chiffon or nylon scarf for each child
   Recording of smoothly flowing music
Directions:

The children swirl, twirl, bend and spin in harmony with the music and the scarves. You may be able to use only a few children at a time, depending upon available space.

Bouncing Ball

Ages: 4-6
Equipment: One or more large balls (8″–10″ diameter)
   Recording of a march or other appropriate music

Directions:

The children bounce and catch the ball in rhythm to the music. This may be an individual activity or used in a group. Experiment and discover what is best with your group using the balls that you have.

The Freeway

Ages: 4-6
Equipment: Hand drum
Directions:

The students move around in a circle as they pretend to be large buses or compact cars on the freeway. The teacher plays the beats on the hand drum to indicate how the students will drive. If the beat is very loud, the student will drive the bus. If the beat is very soft, the student will drive a compact car. The traffic can go faster or more slowly, depending upon the tempo of the drum beat.

All traffic violators are removed from the freeway!

Dancing Kids

Ages: 4-8
Equipment: Recording of rock, jazz, or any music with a strong beat
Directions:

The children stand about the room and respond to the teacher's calls:

"Dance your feet"
"Dance your arms"
"Dance your knees"
"Dance your elbows"
"Dance your legs"
"Dance your hands"
"Dance your body"

Allow a little time between each call and take the time to praise and encourage individual children as you go along.

At the Football Game

Ages: 4-8
Equipment: None
Directions:

Students are directed to stand in a circle. The following verse is chanted. At the conclusion of the verse, a student is chosen to act out any person he might see at a football game (referee, pompon girl, band player, football player, etc.). After each short "act" the verse repeats and play is resumed.

Verse:

I am at a football game,
  a football game, a football game.
I am at a football game,
  guess what I am now!

Variation: The verse may be sung to the tune, "Mary Had a Little Lamb."

For Hands Only

Ages: 4-8
Equipment: Recording of march music
Directions:

The children are seated near the teacher. They rhythmically move their fingers and hands in response to the teacher's calls:

"Clap-ping"	"Ty-ing"
"Hold-ing"	"Scratch-ing"
"Snap-ping"	"Point-ing"
"Fold-ing"	"Squeez-ing"
"Roll-ing"	"Touch-ing"
"Pull-ing"	

The teacher may pause between words while the action continues. Words may also be repeated in the style of a rhythmic chant.

Follow the Leader

Ages: 4-8
Equipment: Recorded music, drum or piano accompaniment
Directions:

The leader marches all about the room with the children following in single file.

* To create a patriotic event, the leader may carry a flag.
* For Halloween, the leader may carry a jack-o'-lantern.
* For springtime, the leader may wave an artificial flower.

For Hands and Arms—Not Legs or Mouth

Ages: 4-8
Equipment: Recording of any rhythmic music
Directions:

The children are standing about the room. They respond rhythmically to the following calls:

"Swing-ing"   "Carry-ing"
"Swim-ming"   "Rest-ing"
"Stretch-ing"   "Sweep-ing"
"Pull-ing"   "Throw-ing"
"Droop-ing"   "Wav-ing"
"Reach-ing"

I Am the Leader

Ages: 4-8
Equipment: Recording of any music
Directions:

One student at a time is chosen as the leader. As the music plays, he creates a movement and the other students follow his lead. After a short time, the teacher points to a new leader and the verse is repeated as play resumes. The choice of music will direct the type of movement.

Verse:

I am the leader; follow, follow me.
You will be what I am doing,
Do it after me.

As Quiet As

Ages: 4-8
Equipment: Several blank cards
            A marking pen
            Recording of "quiet" music
Directions:

Students take turns naming the quietest thing they can think of. As each thing is named, the teacher writes it on a card (or draws a picture of it). During the playing of the recording, the teacher quietly calls (or displays) the various cards and the students quietly dramatize them.

Variation: The game may be used for "tiny" things or "large" things, etc., changing the game from "As Quiet As" to "As Tiny As" or "As Large As."

Directions

Ages: 4-8
Equipment: Drums or a recording of music that has a strong beat
Directions:

The children stand about the room and move in response to the teacher's call.

"Move up"
"Move down"
"Move backward"
"Move forward".
"Move sideways"
"Hands above your head"
"Hands below your knees"
"Hands between your legs"
"Hands in the front"
"Hands in the back"
"Move in a circle"
"Move up and down"
"Stop."

Variation: This game may be played as a "Simon Says " game.

Pantomime

Ages: 4-8
Equipment: Recording of music in a variety of moods and tempi
Directions:

During the following chant, the children silently take their places. They listen quietly to the recording and do an appropriate pantomime.

Verse:

Pantomime, Pantomime all around.
Not a whisper, not a sound.
Take your places; don't say a word.
Pantomime the music that is heard.

About thirty or forty seconds of music is usually enough for each round in this game. At the end of each round, the teacher may want to lead discussion about the various movements used. Children will often want to reveal what they were thinking. Always encourage the children to listen closely to the music so that their movements may "fit."

Pretend and Pose

Ages: 4-8
Equipment: Recording of any music
Directions:

The teacher instructs the students to listen to the short musical selection and imagine what they could "pretend" that would be appropriate. When the selection is played a second time, a student is chosen to dramatize this idea. At the conclusion of the music, students may guess what is being dramatized.

Copy Cat

Ages: 4-8
Equipment: Recording of any music, drum or piano accompaniment
Directions:

The children are seated with the leader at the front. The leader begins to do a rhythmic movement and the others follow. Movements should be changed from time to time to create interest. Suggested movements are: clapping, patting head, patting knee, brushing palms. clapping very loudly, clapping very softly, waving one hand, waving one finger, or nodding head.

A Gallery of Art

Ages: 4-8
Equipment: Recording of any music
            Drawing paper and crayons
Directions:

While sitting at desks or tables, the children listen to a musical composition. Putting their hands in the air they follow the movement of the music as guided by the teacher (flowing lines, circular movements, dots, angles, etc.). Upon hearing the music another time, they make the same motions with crayons on the drawing paper. When the music stops, the picture is complete and ready for display. The music selected for this activity should be generally smooth and flowing. For best results, choose a musical selection that is about three to five minutes long.

Make this a special lesson in art!

ENVIRONMENTAL FANTASY STORIES

Here are some fantasy stories for use with children. What better way to form impressions from contact with the world than for a young child to experience the environment with imagination?

Through free exploration within a story, children's natural curiosity is heightened to experience the unknown. Children learn to understand their environment by what they experience within it.

With the addition of movement and the manipulation of sound-producing materials in the stories, a whole new learning dimension is created.

Prepare the children by directing each one to climb into a private "space-box" where they will be safe from bumps or pushes of others. The teacher should check the "space-box" before the story begins. This little technique can be highly effective in helping children to be mindful of the space of others.

You and your class will have fun with these!

Piano Improvisation

Piano improvisation, though not absolutely necessary, is a great asset to creative movement. If you have a piano and lack keyboard skill, do not worry. The main thing is to practice some simple techniques until you feel comfortable and confident. The following are basic and can be used in the classroom with only a small amount of skill. Do them several times and soon you will feel satisfied with yourself.

Bass Chords:
*   * Slow ones can be spooky stalking music
   * Fast ones can be jumping music

Treble Chords:
   * Slow ones can be resting music
   * Fast ones can be tiptoe music

Scales:
   * Slow ones can be walking music
   * Fast ones can be running music

All of the chords and scales may be used in various rhythm combinations to suggest bouncing, galloping, leaping, etc.

A Music Drama

Ages: 4-6
Equipment: Piano
Directions:

The teacher outlines a very simple story for the children to act out as she accompanies at the piano.

"Let's pretend to be little mice playing all around
  (quick, staccato music)
until the cat comes . . .
  (slow, heavy chords)
and they must scamper to their holes . . ."
  (fast, high sounds).

Other story ideas:

* Corn growing until a bad storm comes
* Children playing in a park until time to go
* Cars on a busy street until the road is closed
* Carpenters building a house until it is finished

Let's Pretend a Trip to the Mountains

Ages: 4-6
Equipment: Piano
The Story:

"Let's pretend a trip! Let's take a hike to the mountain. Put on your good walking shoes. Put your lunch in your backpack . . . Here we go! It's such a lovely day. Let's skip . . . Skipping is fun, but we will get too tired. Let's just walk . . . The mountain gets a little steep here. We must climb, climb, climb. Look at the view. See the pretty flowers over yonder? Let's run over there!

Pick a few flowers to put in my backpack. Mother will like them. Do you think so? Here we must climb up higher. Watch out for the slippery rocks. Climb, climb, climb, climb.

We're getting close to the clouds. Let's have our lunch right here. Find a place to sit. Open your lunch. What kind of sandwich do you have? Yum-Yum. This is good. Just sit and enjoy.

Pick up all of your trash and put it into your backpack and away we go down the mountain. Looks as if we'd better hurry before the rain comes. I think we'd better run.

Time to slow down now because the path is getting rough. Watch your step and walk carefully . . . Here we are at the bottom. Wasn't that a wonderful trip? We must go again sometime."

Let's Pretend a Trip to the Airport

Ages: 4-6
Equipment: Piano
The Story:

"Let's pretend a trip! Let's go to the airport. Close your eyes tightly and you're already there. Keep your eyes closed and see the ticket counter and the ticket man in his uniform. See the ticket lady in her uniform. See all the people with their suitcases and coats.

Look out the window at the airplanes. Open your eyes and see them now. Do you see the big jet right there? It is just beginning to taxi slowly down the runway. Can you be a jet plane and taxi slowly down the runway just like that? . . . Look now, the big jet plane is going up into the air. Do you see? It was on the ground and it rose slowly up into the air? Can you do that? . . . Oh my! Now the jet plane is flying high, high into the clouds. It moves so smoothly and so easily. Can you fly smoothly like that jet?

Well, it's gone out of sight. Look, I see a van carrying suitcases. Wouldn't it be fun to help put all those suitcases on the airplane? So many suitcases! Let's all help. Some are very big. Some are very heavy. Just put these into the baggage compartment. Good! . . . Now the baggage is all loaded. Let's take a look at a helicopter. What big blades it has on the top! See how the blades go around and around. Can you spread your arms and pretend to be a helicopter? Watch out for the others! . . . Would you like to be the pilot of a small airplane? The people said you can be one today if you want to. There are plenty of small planes here. Climb up the steps and get into one. Fasten your safety belt. Look over the control panel. Do you see all of the controls? Now, you can fly your own plane. The control tower will help you with safety. Here we go!

Congratulations! You're back safely on the ground and just in time to return home. Close your eyes tightly, really tightly. Now we're leaving the airport and going home to our own things in our own place. Here we are . . . Open your eyes . . . Airports are such fun!"

Let's Pretend a Trip to an Amusement Park

Ages: 4-6
Equipment: Piano
The Story:

"Let's pretend a trip! Let's go to the amusement park. Close your eyes tightly, really tightly, and here we are. Open your eyes and see! Oh my, this really looks like fun. Where shall we begin? Here with the merry-go-round. Everybody climb on a pony and off we go. The ponies go around and around and up and down, up and down. Oh, I love this.

Well, that certainly was fun. Now it's the racing cars. Everybody find a car. Start your motors. Drive safely everybody . . . What fun! Here we are at the ferris wheel. You may get in a seat with a few friends and go around and around and around. I hope you don't get dizzy.

Better sit for a moment and think. What next? Oh yes, the motor boats. Everybody hop in a boat. Maybe you will need to help a friend. Here go the boats! . . . Now does anybody want to ride the roller coaster? Be prepared for moving high and low, fast and slow. Be-e-e-e-e-e careful!

My, oh my. Do you see any other rides here that you would like to try! What do you see?

Time to go home. Sit down. Close your eyes tightly. Here we are at home again. What a fun day!"

Let's Pretend a Trip to the Zoo

Ages: 4-6
Equipment: Piano
The Story:

"Let's pretend a trip! Let's go visit the zoo! Why, look! We're already at the main gate, so come on in! . . . Here are the elephants big and slow. Let's be elephants just like these. . . . Goodbye elephants.

We want to see the monkeys. Oh, here they are climbing and swinging and jumping and scratching, Let's be monkeys! . . . Goodbye monkeys.

We want to see the giraffes with their long, long necks. I see them already looking over the top of the fence. Now we can see all of the

giraffes. Look, this giraffe is glad to see me. Let's all be giraffes!...
Goodbye giraffes.

Now we must visit the tigers. The big cats are sometimes scary,
but they're nice, too. So big and moving about so quietly. See the
tigers moving quietly on their big soft feet? Let's be tigers! . . .
Goodbye tigers.

The birds are over here. Let's look at the birds. Wow! What a
huge bird cage—bigger than our house. And look at all the birds—
every kind and every color, some flying high, some flying low, some
spreading wings and some flying in circles. Oh, let's be birds like
these!... Goodbye birds.

It's time for us to go. We must leave the zoo now, but we will
come another day. We like the zoo!"

Let's Pretend a Trip to the Shopping Center

Ages: 4-6
Equipment: Piano
The Story:

"Let's pretend a trip! Let's go to the shopping center. The bus is
ready and waiting, so all aboard... This bus ride is sort of bumpy, but
it's fun. We can look out the window and see the whole town.

Here we are at the shopping center. Everybody get out of the bus
and stay with me. We will walk into the mall.

My, we are early shoppers today. We are almost the first ones
here; the mall is nearly empty. That's nice. We can just skip along and
look into all of the shops ... Oh, stop! We must go in this shop. They
have such fun toys. Come on in. Look and look and look. Choose the
toy you want. Now you may take it and play with it for one minute.
Have fun!... Time to put the toys back on the shelf. Say "thank you"
to the shopkeeper. We'll go on down the mall. Oh, look at the antique
cars sitting out here. Wouldn't you love to climb in and pretend to go
for a drive? Let's do it!

Better get back to our shopping. Mother wanted us to try on
some new clothes and here is the clothing store, so in we go! . . .
Everybody find the clothes you want to try on. Will it be a coat? Ski
pants? Blue jeans? Swim suit? A nice shirt? A warm sweater? Find
whatever you wish and try it on for size... Walk around a bit to check
if it is too big or too small. Does it fit just right? Stretch yourself all
around to check.

Get back into your own clothes . . . and continue down the mall. Here are the stairs. Get ready to climb . . . Look at the top of the stairs, just what we need—an ice cream store! Everybody get in line for a cone. What flavor will you have? I will serve you.

M-m-m, good ice cream. But it's melting, so lick it quickly and keep walking back to the bus . . . Here we are! All aboard the bus.

Home again. What a lovely trip!"

A Walk in My Neighborhood

Ages: 4-8
Equipment: Piano (if desired)
Directions:

The students listen to the story and dramatize every action word. The action word is underlined.

"One evening after supper, I asked my Mom, 'May I go for a walk?' 'Sure, and I'll go with you,' she smiled and said. So, I . . . jumped up and down, and wiggled my feet into my shoes. I was so-o-o-o excited. She spun me around like a top, then opened her arms and gave me a great big hug, as we marched out the door. Down the steps we went, left, right, left, right onto the sidewalk. My dog, Fritz, was lying on the ground. I stopped to see if he was awake. He opened his eyes and looked at me. Then he stretched and yawned and shook all over. After a second or two he joined us on our walk. I bent over to pat him on his head. Away we went swinging our arms and letting the breezes blow through our hair. Mom looked over and smiled at me and said, 'You're growing like a weed.' Her smile beamed like a shining star. The trees were swaying gently and the birds were gliding from tree to tree. We passed Mrs. McGillicuddy's house and she was pulling weeds. Her husband was pushing the lawnmower. I saw their son, Jeff, rocking in the swing, back and forth, ever so gently. We waved and went on. As we rounded the corner to go home, I saw my Dad coming home. I jumped high like a frog into the air and ran and ran. As I reached up for him, he threw me into the air and I giggled with delight. We waited for Mom to catch up, she always goes more slowly. Then I rode home on Dad's shoulders bouncing every step of the way."

This Is the Jungle

Ages: 4-8
Equipment: Hand drum
Directions:

Children stand in a circle ready to move and act out the chant given below. The teacher plays a firm, steady rhythm pattern on the drum and chants:

"This is the jungle. This is the jungle.
Here are the elephants. Here are the elephants.
Here are the lions. Here are the lions.
Here are the monkeys. Here are the monkeys.
Here are the zebras. Here are the zebras.
Guess what this is now!"

This Is the Farm

Ages: 4-8
Equipment: Hand drum or piano
Directions:

Children stand about the room ready to move and act out the chant given below. The teacher plays an appropriate accompaniment and chants:

"This is the farm. This is the farm.
Here are the sheep. Here are the sheep.
Here are the horses. Here are the horses.
Here are the rabbits. Here are the rabbits.
Guess what this is now!"

This Is the Ocean

Ages: 4-8
Equipment: Hand drum or piano
Directions:

Children stand about the room ready to move and act out the chant given below. The teacher plays an appropriate accompaniment and chants:

"This is the ocean. This is the ocean.
Here is the beach. Here is the beach.
Here are some crabs. Here are some crabs.
Here are some joggers. Here are some joggers.
Here are some fish a-swimmming. Here are some fish a-swimming.
Here is a boat. Here is a boat.
Guess what this is now!"

This Is the City

Ages: 4-8
Equipment: Hand drum or piano
Directions:

Children stand about the room ready to move and act out the chant given below. The teacher plays an appropriate accompaniment and chants:

"This is the city. This is the city.
Here are the Volkswagens. Here are the Volkswagens.
Here are the trains. Here are the trains.
Here are the buses. Here are the buses.
Here are the airplanes. Here are the airplanes.
Here are the taxis. Here are the taxis . . .
Guess what this is now!"

Our Field Trip

Ages: 4-8
Equipment: Hand drum or piano
Directions:

Just after a field trip, invite the children to take turns acting out (pantomiming) something they saw on the trip. Ask one child to do it several times. While the child is pantomiming, the teacher may begin to provide a rhythmic accompaniment on the drum or piano. After the movement has been identified, all of the class may want to join in doing it together.

Space Trekking

Ages: 4-8
Equipment: Recording appropriate for space travel
Directions:

The teacher leads the students in a discussion of events that might occur on a trip into outer space. The ideas are sequenced and written on cards or on the chalkboard.

The trip begins as the teacher calls the activities for students to pantomime as the trip progresses. Space music provides the background sounds for the trip. Allow a little time between each event so that the children will not be rushed in their pantomime. Let them enjoy their dramatic play!

Variation: Try turning the volume of the music up and down for dramatic effect.

A Walk in the Storm

Ages: 4-8
Equipment: None
Directions:

As the teacher tells this story, the children dramatize the type of step described.

"One day I was slowly walking home from school with my friends. We noticed the clouds beginning to roll in, so we walked faster and faster. We kicked at the dry leaves and leaped high into a pile of raked leaves. We jumped up and down to shake off the leaves and walked on. Soon it began to sprinkle, so we danced on tiptoe through the rain drops. The wind began to blow and move us up the street. As it began to rain, walking through the leaves was much harder because now they were all soggy. We had to take big steps through the puddles to get home quickly."

The story can change as you improvise to use a variety of steps.

The Circus Parade

Ages: 4-8
Equipment: None
The Story:

"At last it is the day of the Circus! We're under the big tent and ready for the show to begin. What a circus parade!

The ringmaster struts in with his baton as he leads the parade...

The pretty ladies parade past, taking tiny steps ...

The ponies trot past wearing feathers in their headdresses ...

The man on stilts takes big wide steps and balances very carefully . . .

Some clowns go very fast on bicycles . . .

Some clowns walk slowly and shake hands with the boys and girls . . .

The horses gallop quickly . . .

High above, the tight rope walker balances back and forth. Careful now . . . *

Time for the show to begin. I love the Circus Parade!"

*You can add more!

GAMES FOR REINFORCING THE STEADY BEAT

Children need an opportunity to express both their physical and emotional nature. The steady beat is the life beat of the music as it is the life of the body pulse.

Using this pulse, the children "become" the steady beat. This is an excellent way to encourage body movement. As an awareness increases of beats in music, the entire body feels the rhythm and an ongoing idea of rhythm is developed.

The responses may be large or small movements; the body may remain stationary or it may be carried through space. Whether stationary or locomotor, it is important to remember that movement should be based upon exploration of sound and space.

Moving is a very personal and intimate experience—an expression of the inner self, an expressive behavior. All children need the opportunity to move in a nonjudgmental, flexible setting. As teachers, can we create such a wholesome classroom?

Pound—Sound

Ages: 4-6
Equipment: None
Directions:

The students are seated in a circle. As they sing or chant the following verse, the action is followed.

Verse One:

Pound, Pound, Pound one fist
Pound it on the ground.

Pound, Pound, Pound, Pound
Make a big loud sound.
Verse Two:
Pound, Pound, Pound two fists, . . . etc.
Verse Three:
Pound, Pound, Pound one foot, . . . etc.
Verse Four:
Pound, Pound, Pound both feet, . . . etc.
(Tune of "Row, Row, Row Your Boat")

Finger March

Ages: 4-6
Equipment: Recording of appropriate music
Directions:

As the march music is played (preferably a staccato or light sound), the fingers tap to the beat. Fingers may march from the toes up the leg and onto the arms or head.

For super fun, draw a face on both of the marching fingers!

Name—Name

Ages: 4-6
Equipment: None
Directions:

The children are seated in a circle. A steady beat is established by patting the legs. The teacher calls the name of each child one by one, and the class repeats the name. Keep the patting at a steady pace and speak the names in rhythm for a very successful class activity!

Hide the Beat

Ages: 4-8
Equipment: Recording of appropriate music
Directions:

The students watch the teacher and imitate actions. As the teacher hides the steady beat movement somewhere on the body (toe, elbow, finger, tongue, eye, etc.), the students imitate the actions. Occasionally the beat will move to another part of the body and the students have to watch carefully to make the change and follow.

What a challenge to find the rhythmic movement wherever it is hidden!

Bean Dip

Ages: 4-8
Equipment: Piano or recording of appropriate music
            Bean bags
Directions:

   The children are seated in a circle. They toss the bean bag to the next child in the circle, passing on the accented beats. When the music ends the child who has the bean bag is the "winner."

Environmental Chant

Ages: 4-6
Equipment: None
Directions:

   The class stands and chants the following verse together.
Verse:
   The patter of my footsteps, (step in rhythm),
   The ringing of a bell, (pretend to pull a bell rope),
   The chug-chug-chug-chug-chug engine, (brush palms together),
   The drip-py, drip-py, faucet, (rock body slowly side to side),
   And still the clock keeps ticking (bend over, clasping the other hand to
      imitate a large pendulum),
   Tick, tock, tick, tock, tick, tock, tick, tock.

Whose Name Is This?

Ages: 4-6
Equipment: None
Directions:

   The teacher claps the rhythm of someone's name and asks, "Whose name is this?" The child whose name it is stands. If several children have names that fit that rhythm, they all may stand together. Another pattern is clapped and another child (or children) stand. Continue in this manner until the rhythm of each name has been clapped. Another day the children can clap with the teacher.

Catch My Tempo

Ages: 4-8
Equipment: Hand drum
Directions:

The teacher plays a steady beat on the drum, while the students march along. The tempo (or speed) of the beat may change and the students listen and respond accordingly.

Variation: One student can move at a time.

Where's the Beat?

Ages: 4-8
Equipment: Recording of appropriate music
Directions:

The teacher (or student-leader) moves a part of his/her body to the beat of the music. The students imitate the actions. The actions change quickly enough to keep a challenge.

Where will the beat be next?

Stop and Go

Ages: 4-8
Equipment: Piano
Directions:

Students march in a circle. The teacher plays march music on the piano. At irregular intervals, the music will stop. When the students hear the music stop, they must stop. When the music begins again the students march until the next stop.

This is a simple idea for a great deal of fun!

Pass and Hold

Ages: 6-8
Equipment: Recording of appropriate music
               Ball
Directions:

Children are organized into lines of approximately six students. The first child in line is given a ball. The children pass the ball on the steady beat to the next player. The pattern is; "pass-pass-pass-pass, hold-2-3-4." Play continues as the students chant the pattern and the ball travels up and down the line.

After some experience, march music may be added to this activity!

Beat Parade

Ages: 6-8
Equipment: Piano or recording of appropriate music
Paper/Pencil
Directions:

The students listen to a recording of a march. As they listen they tap the steady beat. The second time they listen, they draw a tally mark for the beat. For beginning rhythmic notation, playing the march on the piano is recommended.

Moving On

Ages: 6-8
Equipment: Blocks or Sticks
Directions:

Students are seated in a circle. Each student has a block in front of him. On the steady beat the blocks are moved from the center of the person to the center of the next person. Each person passes the block to the next person.

As students become more advanced, each one may pick up the block on his right and move it to his center with his right hand; pick it up with his left and move it to the next person. A pattern of right-center-center-left is established.

Reverse the patterns! Invent your own!

Do it to a drum beat!

Indian Village Messages

Ages: 6-8
Equipment: Drum for each group
Directions:

Students are grouped into small villages. One village sends a beat pattern and the next village echoes the same pattern. When students begin this activity, they may merely count the same number of beats. As they become more proficient, a beat pattern may be echoed.

Great for Thanksgiving activities!

Secret Messages

Ages: 6-8
Equipment: Four drums
Directions:

Players are organized into at least four small groups. One student in the first group sends a rhythm message to Group Two. The receiving person in Group Two echoes it on his drum. He then sends the same message to Group Three and play continues from group to group until it is returned to the first group. The object is to send the same rhythm pattern around all the groups.

What Would Happen If?

Ages: 6-8
Equipment: Drum or resonator bell
Directions:

The teacher plays a pattern on the instrument and a student repeats the pattern. The teacher asks the student, "What would happen if I played it more slowly?" The student plays the same pattern in the new way.

What a challenge to translate the pattern into "faster" or "slower."

What Did I Hear?

Ages: 6-8
Equipment: Rhythm Instruments
Directions:

The student who is "it" hides behind the piano (or where no one can see him) and plays a rhythm pattern. Another student will echo the pattern. If he is correct, he will be "it."

Remember the Pattern

Ages: 6-8
Equipment: None
Directions:

The teacher chants and acts out a four-line pattern and the children repeat.

"Clap, clap, clap, clap
Stamp, stamp, stamp, stamp
Pat, pat, pat, pat
Snap, snap, snap, snap."

After this pattern has been carefully established, the pattern changes to include some rests.

"Clap, clap, clap, rest" (1, 2, 3, 4)
   or
"Clap, rest, clap, clap" (1, 2, 3, 4)

There is no end to the combinations!

Drum Echos

Ages: 6-8
Equipment: Two drums
Directions:

The students are seated in a circle. One drum is given to a student. The teacher plays a simple rhythm pattern and the player echoes it on his instrument. The drum is passed to the next player as play continues.

GAMES FOR LEARNING PATTERNED STEPS

As young children use movement to acquire musical under-standings, it is important that they progress from simple steady beats into more complex patterns. The complexity of the patterns can be varied by repeating the movements, extending the patterns, and requiring the students to remember the patterns.

In these next games a sequence is developed from a single step in response to the music and progresses through hopping, galloping and skipping to steps that will reinforce the patterned dances. Going through a developmental sequence for total mastery is important to the confidence in movement to be gained by any child.

A sequenced pattern that progresses from basic steps is easiest for the students if they say the words, first outwardly and later inwardly as they reinforce the foot actions. For example: "step-step-step-together" is spoken as the feet move the pattern.

This is a good time to watch for auditory or coordination problems. When accompanying the young child you should synchronize the beat to his or her movements. Begin where the child is! Remember that the tempo is faster for smaller children than for the older ones. The little child needs quicker, smaller steps.

The needs for different movements change as a young child matures. Muscular coordination of the four-year-old is good for spontaneous movements at a variety of tempi. Try walking, running, or galloping. By the time a child reaches five years of age, skipping is easier and trotting and marching become more fun. By this time, the child can adjust to the music much more easily also, thus enabling you to work with a greater variety of tempi.

Step 'N' Hold

Ages: 4-6
Equipment: Recording of appropriate music
Directions:

The children will respond to this chant as they step the pattern to a 4/4 meter.

Chant:
"Step - Step - Step - Step,
Hold — Hold — "

Variation: A piano or recording may accompany the movements.

Long 'N' Short

Ages: 4-6
Equipment: Piano or recording of appropriate music
Directions:

The children will respond to the pattern of a long step followed by a short step as they move to a 6/8 meter.

Chant:
"Long - short, Long - short"

This is a pre-gallop step which leads into a step-close pattern.

What Did I Do?

Ages: 4-6
Equipment: None
Directions:

The student is expected to remember a stepped pattern after seeing it performed one time, and then be able to repeat it.

Begin with simple step and step-hop patterns.

Walk My Way

Ages: 4-6
Equipment: Piano or recording of appropriate music
Directions:

The children will mirror the movement of the teacher as they follow a variety of rhythmic steps in combination. Each step should be repeated for at least four measures to avoid confusion.

Getting Into a Circle

Ages: 4-6
Equipment: None
Directions:

Students follow the leader into and around a circle. This is a neat way to form a circle with a group of young children.

(Song sung to the folk tune: Old Joe Clark)

Round, round, round you go,
Round you go my dear.
Round, round round you go
And we'll stop right here.

Tiptoe Raindrops

Ages: 4-6
Equipment: Recording of appropriate music
Directions:

The students perform a light staccato step-step pattern on their tiptoes in response to the music. Pretending to dance through rain drops is fun!

Funny Freeze

Ages: 4-6
Equipment: Piano chords or simple recording
Directions:

As the music is played, the children will walk to the steady beat. When the music stops each child freezes. They will try to stop in a funny position. This is a good activity to reinforce careful listening as well as the direction word "freeze." To "freeze" means to stop all movement.

Smooth Move

Ages: 4-6
Equipment: Recording of appropriate music
Directions:

The children listen to some softly flowing music. Without using their feet, they move their bodies to the musical phrases.

Try adding beautiful scarves for a variety!

Step My Pattern

Ages: 4-6
Equipment: Hand drum
Directions:

The children listen to a rhythm pattern and then upon the second hearing, step with the beat. This is good for a "one-at-a-time" activity.

Some patterns are:

Try using contrasting timbre for variety!

Sidewalk Steps

Ages: 4-6
Equipment: None
Directions:

Children love to walk on sidewalks, taking great care to avoid getting caught by the cracks! Chant this verse with them as they pretend to walk on the sidewalk.

Verse:

Let us take giant steps over cracks in the sidewalk,
Let us take great strides so we don't get caught.
Let us walk backwards with the same big steps
And never, never, never get caught.

Trotting Pony

Ages: 4-6
Equipment: Recording of appropriate music
Directions:

The students take slow steps with knees high as they pretend to be walking ponies in response to the music. They can move as a trotting pony by raising knees high. Perhaps they would rather be a galloping pony in response to a change in music.

Indians

Ages: 4-8
Equipment: Hand drum or piano
Directions:

The students become Indians by using a step-hold pattern in response to a drum beat. The right foot begins the step/hold. On the hold beat the knee flexes. Then the left foot does the same pattern.

Piano music of an Indian dance is fun to add with the drum.

Galloping Ponies in the Ring

Ages: 4-8
Equipment: Piano or recording of appropriate music
Directions:

The students form a circle and gallop as the music is played. This gallop step is a step-together pattern that is performed in a forward direction. Changing the tempo from fast to slow helps reinforce listening skills.

A few students at a time may be chosen to avoid confusion!

Mechanical Man

Ages: 4-8
Equipment: Piano or recording of appropriate music.
Directions:

The students are in a line and use a sideward step-close pattern. As students become more proficient in this sideward step they can combine it with other step patterns into a routine.

Choose heavy ponderous music and you will have some wonderful mechanical men!

Follow, Follow Me

Ages: 4-8
Equipment: None
Directions:

The children will chant the verse with the teacher and then follow the pattern that is given.

Verse:

Follow, follow, follow me
Do what I do after me:
Walk, walk, walk, walk

Jump, jump, jump, jump

Sway,   Sway.

The type of action can vary to include any step or combination of step patterns.

Who Can?

Ages: 4-8
Equipment: Recording of appropriate music
Strips of colored paper
Directions:

The game begins with children in a circle. As the piano or record is played, the student moves to the beat. It might be a steady beat such as march, run, jump, hop or leap; or if the music indicates, it might be an uneven beat such as a gallop, slide or skip.

As the children pass by the teacher, a strip of colored paper is given to each child indicating skill in accomplishing the movement. A red paper may mean "excellent"; a blue paper may mean "needs improving."

This is a quick and easy way for an on-the-spot evaluation of the skill of each child during a large group experience.

Later, the teacher can record the evaluation by using the color-coded strips held by the children. A teacher's aid is well used here, also.

Circle Shapes

Ages: 4-8
Equipment: Paper shapes of circles, squares, rectangles, and triangles cut from a variety of colors
Directions:

The children stand in a circle. Each child has a paper shape. As the teacher sings the song, the child who has the requested shape holds it high into the air.

Song: (Tune: If You're Happy and You Know It)

"If you have a blue triangle hold it in the air.
If you have a green circle hold it up.
If you have a yellow square hold it high in the air.
If you have a red rectangle hold it up."

Hokey Pokey Colors

Ages: 4-8
Equipment: Paper shapes of circles, squares, rectangles, and triangles cut from a variety of colors
Directions:

The children stand in a circle. Each child is given a colored shape to hold. As the song "Hokey-Pokey" is sung, call a shape and color for recognition. When the color or shape is sung, the child holding that one holds it high into the air.

Song:

"You put your red circle in
You put your red circle out
You put your red circle in and you shake it all about.
You do the Hokey-Pokey and you turn yourself about.
That's what it's all about!"

This is fun as a follow-up to the game "Circle Shapes."

The Bunny's Hop

Ages: 4-8
Equipment: Recording of the "Bunny Hop"
Directions:

This is a story that includes a variety of steps woven in a short drama. As the story progresses, the children dramatize the actions.

List of Characters:

Mother Bunny	Messenger Bunny
Bunny Children	King Bunny
Queen Bunny	Court Bunny

One day as Mother Bunny was cleaning her hutch and the Bunny children were playing close by, a messenger from the Bunny King marched past. He stopped right in front of their door. He read a proclamation in a loud-clear voice, "Hear ye, Hear ye, the Bunny King is having a huge dance for all of his friends. Please come." Then he marched on. You can imagine how excited all the Bunnies were. They leaped and jumped and ran in little circles. They were so excited. "Hold it, just one munute," said Mother Bunny. "We cannot go until the house and yard are tidy." "Let's all work together," said the children. They lined up and played follow-the-leader through the yard and into the house. While some bunnies reached up very high and swayed back and forth cleaning the ceiling; some skated around and dusted the floor. When the house was sparkling clean they ran quickly through the yard. They bent over very low and picked up all of the toys. By this time they were so tired they sat down to rest a spell.

After a bit, Mother Bunny said, "Let's go." So they brushed their teeth and started across the field. Over a fence, under the trees, through the meadow they went. They laughed and sang as they skipped, then jogged, then ran and walked—quickly at first and then more slowly.

At last they came to the Palace of the Bunny King. They were just in time! They joined in the big party and met a lot of new friends. The Bunny King said, "Let's all dance together." So, of course, they did the Bunny Hop. What a glorious day!

Simplified Version of the Bunny Hop:

Right foot out; Right foot in;
Right foot out; Right foot in;
Left foot out; Left foot in;
Left foot out; Left foot in
Hop forward; Hop backward
Hop, Hop, Hop.

Swing and Sway

Ages: 4-8
Equipment: Piano or recording of appropriate music
Directions:

"Bend from the waist and swing arms across the body; around to the ground and hang limply; then raise back up and swing from the shoulders." A slow walk can be added as students pretend to be anything from elephants to rag dolls.

This pattern works well with a 6/8 beat.

Musical Hopscotch

Ages: 6-8
Equipment: Piano
Directions:

The students take turns performing this pattern as they pretend to be on a hopscotch grid.

"Hop - feet apart - feet together - hop"

This pattern works well with a slower 4/4 beat.

Hula Hop

Ages: 6-8
Equipment: Hula Hoops
Directions:

The hula hoops are placed in a line. A step-hop pattern is used as the students step into the hoop and hop, then step into the next hoop and hop, etc.

What fun and a real challenge to add music to!

Skippity Skip

Ages: 6-8
Equipment: Piano or recording of appropriate music
Directions:

An advanced step-hop pattern evolves into a skipping pattern. The students skip to the speed of the music. A careful watch should be made for children who have difficulty skipping forward.

Vary the tempo and challenge their ears!

SINGING GAMES

Singing games are the cultural property of young children. No young child's musical experience would be complete without them. The fun of skipping in a circle, joining hands, moving as one in a group—all are the special thrilling qualities of singing games. On the following pages is a collection of singing games that are especially chosen for their universal appeal and familiarity. Use them all and witness the wonder of young children growing to love the things we already cherish.

England   Ring Around the Rosy

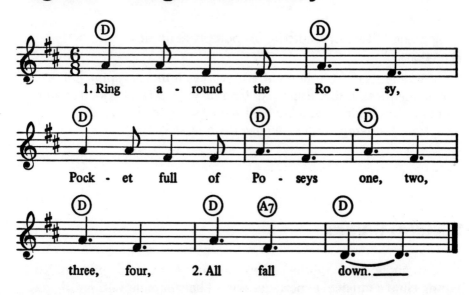

Ages: 4-6
Formation: Circle with hands joined.
Directions:

1. Circle left.
2. Everyone falls down.

England   The Muffin Man

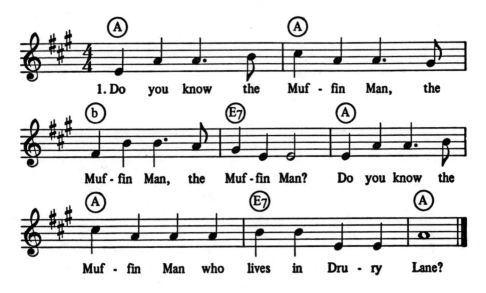

1. Do   you   know   the   Muf - fin   Man,   the   Muf - fin   Man,   the   Muf - fin   Man?   Do   you   know   the   Muf - fin   Man   who   lives   in   Dru - ry   Lane?

Verse 2:

Yes, I know the Muffin Man, the Muffin Man, the Muffin Man.
Yes, I know the Muffin Man who lives in Drury Lane

Ages: 4-6
Formation: Circle with hands joined.
             "It" stands in the center.

Directions:

1. Circle left.
2. "It" chooses a partner and they skip together.

England   The Mulberry Bush

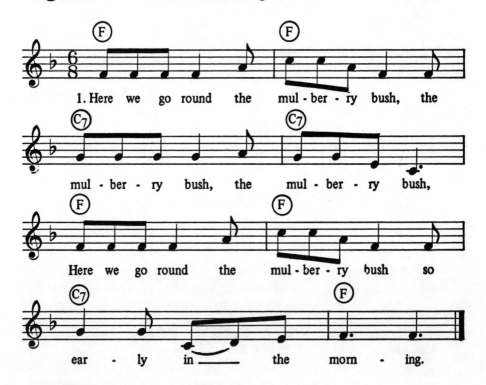

1. Here we go round the mul-ber-ry bush, the
mul-ber-ry bush, the mul-ber-ry bush,
Here we go round the mul-ber-ry bush so
ear-ly in the morn-ing.

Ages: 4-6
Formation: Circle with hands joined.
Directions:

1. Circle left.
2. Stop and dramatize actions of each verse.

**Additional verses:

This is the way we wash our face . . .
This is the way we comb our hair . . .
This is the way we brush our teeth . . .
This is the way we tie our shoes . . .
This is the way we drink our milk . . .
This is the way we walk to school . . .

**Join hands and repeat the first verse as a finale!

England   London Hill

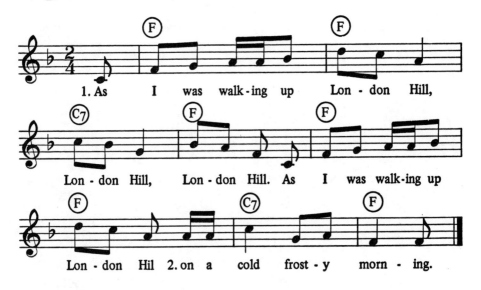

1. As I was walk-ing up Lon-don Hill, Lon-don Hill, Lon-don Hill. As I was walk-ing up Lon-don Hil 2. on a cold frost-y morn-ing.

Verse 2: I button my coat when the North Wind blows. . . .

Verse 3: I put on my hat in case it snows. . . .

Ages: 4-6

Formation: Circle with hands joined.

Directions:

1. Circle left, dramatizing words throughout.
2. Hug yourself vigorously each time on the last line.

**Create some new verses!

England   Sing a Song of Sixpence

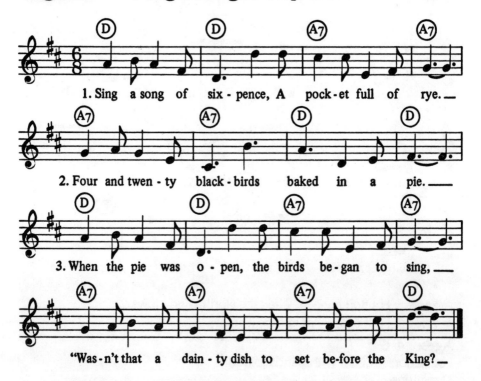

1. Sing a song of six - pence, A pock - et full of rye. ___

2. Four and twen - ty black - birds baked in a pie. ___

3. When the pie was o - pen, the birds be - gan to sing, ___

"Was - n't that a dain - ty dish to set be-fore the King? ___

The King was in his counting house a-counting out his money.
The Queen was in the parlor eating bread and honey.
The Maid was in the garden a-hanging out the clothes.
When down came a blackbird and pecked her on the nose!

Ages: 4-6
Formation: Circle with hands joined.
Directions:

1. All circle left.
2. Children stop and stretch arms toward center of circle.
3. Raise arms upwards and flap them like birds'.
4. Children dramatize actions of each character.

England   Looby Loo

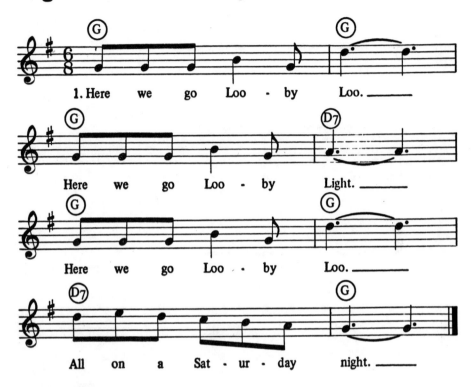

Ages: 4-6

Formation: Circle with hands joined.

Directions:

1. Circle left.

2. Children stop and dramatize each verse of the song.

***Additional verses:*

I put my right hand in . . .
(and shake it all around)
I put my left hand in . . .
I put my right foot in . . .
I put my left foot in . . .
I put my whole self in . . .

**Repeat the first section after each new verse.

Ireland   Here We Go, Santy Malone

Ages: 4-6
Formation: Circle with hands joined.
Directions:

    1. Circle left.

    2. Do the action suggested by the words for each verse.

  **Create additional verses.*

    Pat your hands on your shoulders . . .

    Tap your hands on your back bone . . .

    Stamp your feet on the floor . . .

    **Repeat the first section after each verse.

United States   Clap Your Hands

Ages: 4-6

Formation: Circle with hands not joined.

Directions:

1. Stand still and clap the beat throughout the first section.
2. Raise both hands; wiggle fingers and slowly turn the body around.

**Repeat the first section!

England   London Bridge

Ages: 4-8

Formation: Two children (one is Gold; the other Silver) join hands to form a bridge. Other children line up, single file, to pass under the bridge.

Directions:

Children walk under the bridge as the song is sung. At the words, "My fair lady," the bridge falls. The child who is caught is asked to choose Silver or Gold and stand behind the one chosen. The game continues until all children are caught. At the end a tug-of-war may be played between the Gold and Silver lines.

England   The Farmer in the Dell

Verse 2: The Farmer takes a Wife . . .
Verse 3: The Wife takes a Child . . .
Verse 4: The Child takes a Nurse . . .
Verse 5: The Nurse takes a Dog . . .
Verse 6: The Dog takes a Cat . . .
Verse 7: The Cat takes a Rat . . .
Verse 8: The Rat takes the Cheese . . .
Verse 9: The Cheese stands alone . . .

Ages: 4-8
Formation: Circle with hands joined and the "Farmer" in the center.
Directions:

The words are dramatized by each new character choosing another character. At the end, all of the "characters" return to the circle except for the Cheese who "stands alone."

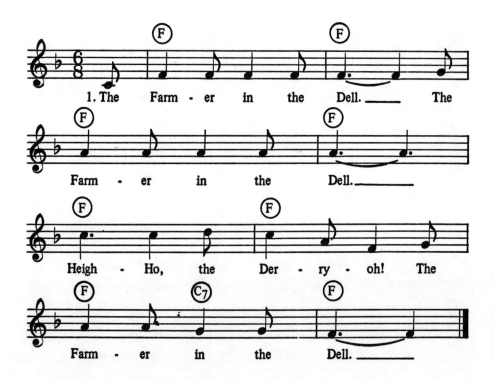

**Halloween Variation of "The Farmer in the Dell"

1. The Witch on Halloween ...
2. The Witch takes a Ghost ...
3. The Ghost takes a Jack-o'-lantern ...
4. The Jack-o'-lantern takes a Cat ...
5. The Cat takes a Skeleton ...
6. The Skeleton takes a Bone ...
7. The Bone stands alone ...

Ozark Mountains Jim Along Josie

Verse 2: Skip along, skip along, Josie, Hey . . .
Verse 3: Jump along, Jump along, Josie, Hey . .
Verse 4: Run along, run along, Josie, Hey . .
Verse 5: Creep along, creep along, Josie, Hey . . .

Ages: 4-8
Formation: Circle with hands not joined.
Directions:

1. Children move clockwise about the circle, adjusting the movement to dramatize the words

United States   Shoo, Fly!

Ages: 4-8
Formation: Circle with hands joined.
Directions:

1. Circle moves to the left
2 Circle moves to center and back with all hands held high.

England   A Tisket, A Tasket

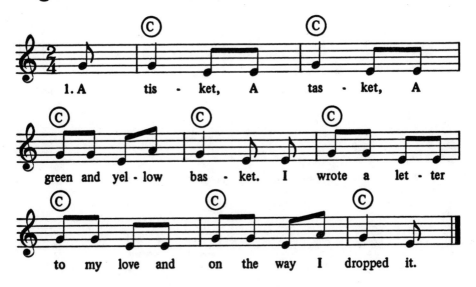

Verse 2: I dropped it; I dropped it and on the way I dropped it.

Verse 3: A little boy (girl) picked it up and put it in his (her) pocket.

Ages: 4-8

Formation: Circle with hands not joined. "It" is standing outside the circle holding the "letter" (use any small paper).

Directions:

1. "It" skips around the circle.
2. "It" drops letter behind another player and continues skipping around the circle once more.
3. The new player picks up the "letter" and begins to skip around the circle.

Kentucky   The Paw-Paw Patch

Verse 2: Come on boys, let's all go find her (3 times)
Way down yonder in the Paw-Paw Patch!

Verse 3: Picking up Paw-Paws, putting them in a basket (3 times)
Way down yonder in the Paw-Paw Patch!

Ages: 4-8
Formation: A line of boys facing a line of girls.
Partners are designated and stand opposite.
Directions:

1. Head girl skips around both lines of dancers and back to place.
2. All boys skip around girls' line and back to place.
3. Head couple joins inside hands, skips halfway around the circle to the foot of the formation where they stop and form a two-handed arch. Other couples follow them and proceed under the arch into a position as at first.

United States   Hokey-Pokey

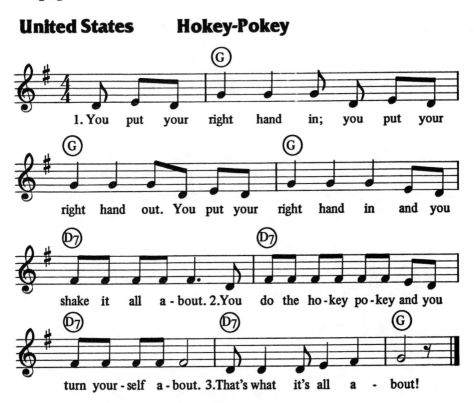

1. You put your right hand in; you put your right hand out. You put your right hand in and you shake it all a-bout. 2. You do the ho-key po-key and you turn your-self a-bout. 3. That's what it's all a-bout!

Ages: 4-8
Formation: A circle with hands not joined.
Directions:

1. Dramatize the words for each verse.
2. Raise hands high; shake fingers; turn around in place.
3. Face center of the circle and clap the rhythm of the words.

**Additional verses:

You put your left hand in . . .
You put your right foot in . . .
You put your left foot in . . .
You put your head in . . .
You put your whole self in . . .

Iowa   Pop! Goes the Weasel

Ages: 4-8
Formation: Circle with hands joined.
Directions:

1. Circle left.
2. Swing the joined hands.
3. Clap or stamp on "pop" each time.

Virginia   Hey, Betty Martin

Ages: 6-8
Formation: Every player needs some space about him.
The group may or may not be arranged in a circle.
Directions:

1. All players tiptoe about the room.
2. Children stop in place and do the action mentioned.

**Repeat first two lines after each verse.
**Create new verses for Part 2 such as:

Jump with me . . .   Run with me . . .
Clap with me . . .   Skip with me . . .

United States   All Around the Kitchen

Ages: 6-8

Formation: Circle with hands not joined.

Directions:

1. Children move clockwise around the circle taking care to walk in a funny "chicken" style.
2. Dramatize the words of the song on phrases three, four and five.

Sweden   How D'ya Do, My Partner?

1. How d'ya do, my part - ner? 2. How d'ya do to - day? —

3. Will you dance in the cir - cle? I will show you the way.

4. La la la la la la. La la la la la. —

La la la la la la. La la la la la la.

Ages: 6-8
Formation: Circle with hands not joined.
"It" stands in the center.

Directions:

1. "It" skips to a child in the circle.
2. They shake hands.
3. They skip around inside the circle.
4. They continue skipping while all children clap hands in rhythm.

England   Did You Ever See a Lassie?

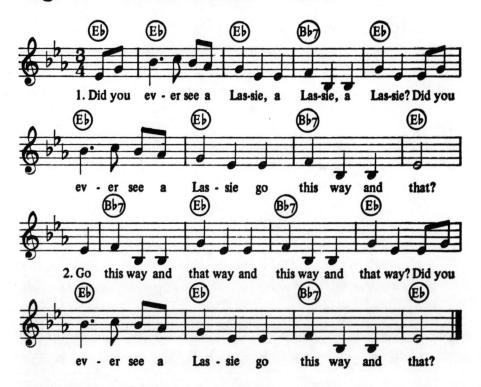

Ages: 6-8

Formation: Circle with hands not joined.
                 "It" is a part of the circle.

Directions:

1. Children stand in place and sing.
2. "It" begins to make a motion and all others follow. (Moving hands, arms, legs, feet, head, etc.)

**Try to think of lots of different motions each time.

England Oats and Beans and Barley Grow

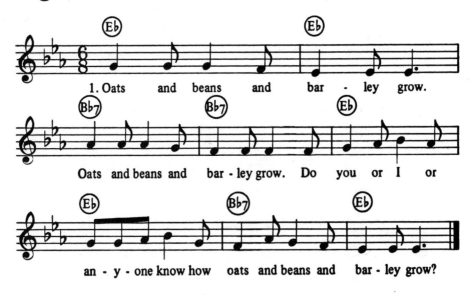

1. Oats and beans and bar - ley grow.
Oats and beans and bar - ley grow. Do you or I or
an - y - one know how oats and beans and bar - ley grow?

Verse 2: First the farmer sows the seed;
Then he stands and takes his ease,
Stamps his foot and claps his hand
And turns around to view the land.

Verse 3: Waiting for a partner,
Waiting for a partner,
Open the ring and take one in
Oats and beans and barley grow.

Verse 4: La la la la la la, la la la la la la,
La la la la la la la la la la la la la la la la.

Ages: 6-8
Formation: Circle with hands joined and the "farmer" in the center.
Directions:

1. Circle to the left around the "farmer."
2. All stop and dramatize the words.
3. Children join hands and swing arms gently while farmer chooses a partner.
4. Farmer and partner skip around the circle.

Texas   **Bluebird, Bluebird**

Ages: 6-8

Formation: Circle with hands joined
"Bluebird" in the center.

Directions:

1. Children all raise joined hands high and the "bluebird" skips
   in and out of the circle under the arms.
2. "Bluebird" chooses a partner and they skip together.

Mississippi   Rise, Sally, Rise

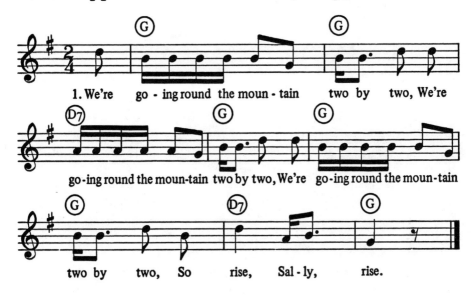

1. We're go - ing round the moun - tain two by two, We're go-ing round the moun-tain two by two, We're go-ing round the moun-tain two by two, So rise, Sal - ly, rise.

Verse 2: Let me see you make a statue, two by two (3 times),
So rise, Sally, rise.

Verse 3: That's a mighty fine statue, two by two (3 times)
So rise, Sally, rise.

Verse 4: Let me see you make another one, two by two, (3 times),
So rise, Sally, rise.

Verse 5: That's a very fine statue, two by two (3 times),
So rise, Sally, rise.

Ages: 6-8
Formation: Partners standing side by side with one hand joined.
Partners may be standing in a circle.

Directions:

1. Partners join hands and skip "round the mountain."
2. Partners join right hands and swing each other around.
3. Partners let go and land in a pose. Freeze the pose until the end of the verse.
4. Motions as in verse two.
5. Motions as in verse three.

**Caution: This game requires an extra amount of space.

United States   Old Brass Wagon

1. Cir - cle to the left, the old Brass Wag - on,

Cir-cle to the left, the old Brass Wag - on, Cir-cle to the left, the

old Brass Wag - on. You're the one, my dar - ling.

Verse 2: Circle to the Right, the Old Brass Wagon, etc.
Verse 3: Come to the Middle, the Old Brass Wagon, etc.
Verse 4: Clap your hands, the Old Brass Wagon, etc.

Ages: 6-8
Formation: Circle with hands joined.
Directions: Follow directions of the words in each verse.

England   Round and Round the Village

Verse 2: Go in and out the windows . . .

Verse 3: Go forth and face a partner . . .

Ages: 6-8

Formation: Circle with hands joined.
              "It" is in the center.

Directions:

1. Circle left.
2. Children stop, raise hands high and "It" weaves in and out of the circle.
3. "It" stops in front of another child.
   They may exchange places for another round.

Virginia   Bow, Bow, Bow, Belinda

1. Bow, Bow, Bow, Be-lin-da. Bow, Bow, Bow, Be-lin-da.

Bow, Bow, Bow, Be-lin-da. Won't you be my part-ner?

Verse 2: One hand 'round, oh, Belinda . . .
Verse 3: Other hand 'round, oh, Belinda . . .
Verse 4: Both hands 'round, oh, Belinda . . .

Ages: 6-8
Formation: A large circle with each child facing a partner.
Directions:

1. Bow slowly to partner several times.
2. Take partner's hand and swing.
3. Take partner's other hand and swing.
4. Take partner in a two-handed swing.

Virginia   Jingle at the Window

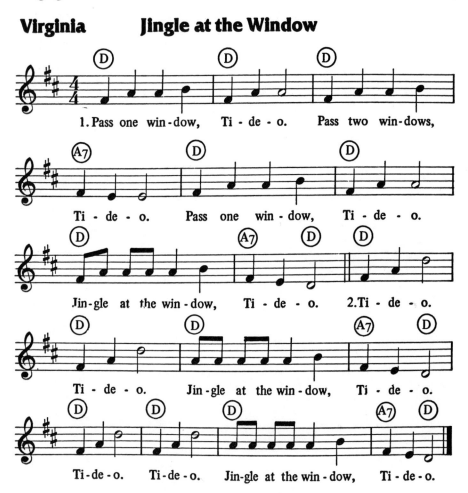

1. Pass one win-dow, Ti-de-o. Pass two win-dows, Ti-de-o. Pass one win-dow, Ti-de-o. Jin-gle at the win-dow, Ti-de-o. 2. Ti-de-o. Ti-de-o. Jin-gle at the win-dow, Ti-de-o. Ti-de-o. Ti-de-o. Jin-gle at the win-dow, Ti-de-o.

Ages: 6-8

Formation: A single circle, girls in front of partners, facing counter-clockwise. Each child places left hand on the left shoulder of the child in front of him.

Directions:

1. The group moves around the circle in time to the music.
2. Partners swing.

Variation: At the end of each dance, the boys may step to the next girl, thus having new partners for each round.

Part Two

GAMES FOR MELODY

Listening to Melody 79
Reading Melody 84
Writing Melody 89

Children naturally enjoy simple melodies. They like to sing them, hum them and play them. Melodies are a part of their immediate world.

The preschooler enjoys exploring and manipulating materials while he works by himself or in parallel learning situations. As a child matures, he or she begins to follow directions and take an interest in other boys and girls. At this time the type of game structure can evolve into group participation or simple competition. The child just beginning school has developed a sense of time and duration. He or she can repeat long sequences, has a carry-over from day to day, is capable of abstractions, and will have an idea of "yesterday" and "tomorrow."

Montessori's "doing-learning" philosophy applies beautifully to the learning of melody. The young child should be encouraged to create from his or her own environment when beginning to develop a perception of melody. Many experiences in listening and experimenting with sound need to be provided as the foundation for reading and writing music. Games and actually working with objects are important in developing a physical expression of an intrinsic music concept such as melody.

Music should never be considered a spectator sport for young children. They must be continuously and actively involved in their own learning processes.

LISTENING TO MELODY

Young children need to be carefully trained in discriminative listening and guided in the interpretation of what they hear. Children from four to eight years old come to school with a considerable background in music. From these experiences, they have already developed musical preferences. They already "know" musical sounds and how they feel about them. They have spent many hours hearing and watching their families respond to music of many styles and settings. Music has already set the stage for visual and verbal communications. From watching television they have mixed the visual stimulation with sound and understand how music sets the mood, the action, or identification of characters. Their internal responses have become an automatic process which is not actually related to the fine art of "listening" or "responding" to music as a basic concept.

Children learn to feel and experience simple musical patterns as they listen carefully to sounds. A gradual understanding of the organization of musical symbols develops as young students learn to discriminate patterns of sound. A constant check must be made by the teacher to know what a student is hearing.

So many other things are learned through musical activities at this early age. Students obtain practice in concentration, in following directions, and in group cooperation within a framework of creative expression and enjoyment of music.

The Note Family

Ages: 4-6
Equipment: Diatonic bells
Directions:

The teacher reads the story and the students follow the directions.

"Once upon a time, there was a Note Family. They were all named 'C.' They all sounded like this. Everywhere they went, people knew them because they were all alike. They all looked alike and they all sounded alike.

"One day Mr. C said, 'I'm tired of always sounding like everyone else. I am going to change my name to 'D.' And so he did. After he changed his name to 'D' he sounded like this. His new sounding name made him so happy that he played it as he marched, tah-tah; he played it as he ran (tee-tee-tee-tee); and he played it while he skipped (tah-tee-tah-tee). The idea began to catch on among other members of the family."

(The story continues until the students are playing the C Major Scale).

Variation: Place notes on flannel board or floor staff.

Music Has Feeling

Ages: 4-6
Equipment: Three selected pictures
Piano or recordings
Directions:

The teacher displays three pictures that depict contrasting feelings and different situations, such as a wild animal, a baby sleeping, and children playing. Music appropriate for each picture is played (on piano or recording) and the students choose the picture that feels as if it agrees with the music.

Loud/Soft Melodies

Ages: 4-6
Equipment: Piano, recorded examples, or melody instruments
Directions:

The students listen to a short melody that varies from loud to soft. If the melody is loud, they open their arms wide. If the melody is soft, they hold their arms close to their bodies.

High/Low Hands

Ages: 4-6
Equipment: A melody instrument
Directions:

The students position their hands at the waist as the verse is chanted. After the verse two pitches are played. If the second pitch is higher, the hands go up into the air; if the second pitch is lower the hands go down to the floor. As students become more mature listeners, the intervals can become smaller.

Verse:
My hands can show a melody
Which might be high or low,
Everyone can help me now,
Listen as we go.

Hands Up High

Ages: 4-6
Equipment: None
Directions:

Chant the following rhyme on appropriate pitch (high, middle or low) and do the suggested motions.

Hands up high to the sky.
Hands down low; touch your toe.
Hands in the middle; I'm fit as a fiddle!

Where Is the Melody?

Ages: 4-6
Equipment: Rhythm and Melody Instruments
Directions:

One player is blindfolded. A melody instrument and a rhythm instrument are played on opposite sides of the room. If the teacher says, "Where is the melody?" the student walks toward the melody instrument sound. If the teacher says, "Where is the rhythm?" the student walks toward the rhythm sound.

Vary this by using several instruments in each category or by having instruments move about the room.

Can You Hear My Step?

Ages: 4-6
Equipment: Step bells
Directions:

The teacher plays a melody (8-12 notes) on the step bells. When the pattern moves by step, the students listen and walk with their feet. When the melody goes by skip, they stop and raise their hands high into the air.

Being a Melody

Ages: 6-8
Equipment: Piano or bells
Directions:

One child stands on the middle of the floor staff. As the teacher plays a simple melody on piano or bells, the child moves appropriately to the music, i.e., upward on the staff for an ascending melody, downward on the staff for a descending melody, across the staff for a repeating melody.

Melody Groups

Ages: 6-8
Equipment: Piano or recordings
Directions:

Children are divided into four groups, each in a designated area. The teacher assigns a certain song or melody to each group. When they hear their melody on piano or recording they are to dance about in a circle. When they don't hear their melody, they are to stand still.

This activity can be used in varying degrees of difficulty depending upon the melodies selected. Familiar tunes are easiest; abstract melodies hardest. An orchestral composition with clearcut form and clear-cut melodies may be used in this manner with older children. Try movements from "The Children's Symphony" by Harl MacDonald.

Echo My Pattern

Ages: 6-8
Equipment: Bells or piano
Directions:

As the teacher plays a simple tune on either bells or piano, the student sings it back using neutral sounds like "Da." The response can be from a single student or the group response.

Variation: For a more advanced class, try playing the same pattern on the bells for the students to play back on their bells.

Which Is Different?

Ages: 6-8
Equipment: Resonator bells
Directions:

The teacher plays three tonal patterns on the resonator bells (two patterns alike and one different). It is the task of the students to decide which pattern was different.

This activity is good for a team game with scorekeeping or as an individual-response activity.

Is It the Same?

Ages: 6-8
Equipment: Bells or piano
Directions:

The teacher plays two short tonal patterns on the bells or piano. The students listen to the patterns to determine if they sounded the same or different. As students become better listeners, the patterns may become more similar.

Variation: The students may create the patterns.

READING MELODY

Learning to read music is a complex process involving the decoding of written symbols. It involves a need to concentrate, a good memory, and the ability to understand abstract concepts. This learning process cannot be rushed into nor dealt with in a haphazard fashion. It is an outgrowth of many careful listening experiences. It is only as a young child begins to break the code of symbolic notation that he can learn to read music.

This gradual process occurs simultaneously with the development of language skills. Listening to musical patterns, and the complex integration of the senses (which is required to read symbolic notation), can help improve other skills in language. The student at early school age will enjoy a team game and is motivated by gentle rivalry.

Piaget sums the music reading process succinctly ". . . even in order to understand we have to invent, or that is, to reinvent, because we can't start from the beginning again. But I would say that anything is only understood to the extent that it is reinvented."

Line Up

Ages: 4-6
Equipment: Floor staff
Directions:

Each student in turn is directed to take a walk on a specific line of the floor staff.

Variation: Walk on a specific space!

Climbing Note Mountain

Ages: 4-6
Equipment: Set of melody cards
Cardboard or plastic figure of a person (3" is fine)
Directions:

Student draws one melody card and places the plastic figure on the first note. Then, moving the figure from left to right, he or she must chant or sing the appropriate phrase: "the man is climbing up," "the man is climbing down," or "the man is staying the same."

Reading a Hand Song

Ages: 4-6
Equipment: None
Directions:

The teacher leads the children in singing a "Hand Song." The teacher's hands represent the following;

"High": hands above head
"Middle": hands just above waist
"Low": hands at knees

Children may sing words "high," "middle," or "low" on pitches corresponding to Sol, Mi and Do. (Some teachers may prefer to use words Sol, Mi and Do, with the traditional hand signs.) After a little experience at singing a hand song, the children will enjoy leading the song with each child taking a turn.

Step Bell Composition

Ages: 4-6
Equipment: Step bells
Prepared Chart
Directions:

Prepare a simple chart (or chalk board) using notes something like this.

High	♩	♩					♩
Middle			♩		♩		
Low				♩			

As you point along the chart, left to right, the student will play the appropriate bells. Obviously, any bells will do, but step bells function graphically here because they appear like a ladder: High, Middle, Low.

A Walk on the Stair

Ages: 4-6
Equipment: Step bells
Directions:

As the teacher plays a pattern on the bells, the question will be asked, "Did I walk carefully on every single step?" or "Did I go down the steps skipping?"

A student may "walk on the stairs." Ask, "How are you walking on the stairs?" The pattern used may be written on the chalk board to read afterward.

Feel and Find Box

Ages: 6-8
Equipment: Three-dimensional music symbol cards
Directions:

Prepare pairs of three-dimensional music symbol cards with felt or sandpaper figures. Place all cards (shuffled) into a box. The object is for the child to find matched pairs of notes, note patterns, or other musical symbols without looking at the cards. He or she must use only the sense of touch.

This is great for a learning center.

Arrows on Bells

Ages: 6-8
Equipment: Prepared chart or chalk board
                   Six or more sets of diatonic bells
Directions:

Prepare a chart or chalk board from which children may play the diatonic bells, using arrows as the notation symbol. Ascending arrow means upward glissando; descending arrow means downward glissando; horizontal arrow means melody moving on a repeated tone.

Display these three symbols and point randomly to them.
Children will play bells as indicated.

Point and Say

Ages: 6-8
Equipment: Melody pattern on chalk board
Directions:

As the melody pattern is studied, the teacher points to each note,
one by one and the appropriate phrase is chanted for each note.

Phrases:

This note moves by step
This note moves up (down) by a skip
This note is a repeat
This note is the end.

Which One Am I?

Ages: 6-8
Equipment: Set of melody cards
Directions:

Two or three melody cards are displayed. Questions are asked
by the students as they try to discover which one melody pattern the
teacher has chosen. Students may ask such questions as: "Does the
pattern move by steps?" "Does it move upward?" "Does it move
downward?"

Variation: Teacher gives clues for student to identify the pattern
chosen.

Another variation: Students take turns being the "teacher" in
this game.

Which One Do You Hear?

Ages: 6-8
Equipment: Set of melody cards
Directions:

Two melody cards are displayed. The teacher plays a pattern.
The students respond by telling which they heard. A third melody
card may be added as skill is developed.

Melody Matching

Ages: 6-8
Equipment: Set of melody cards
Bells, recorder, or piano
Directions:

Three melody cards are displayed, two of which are alike and one of which is different. The student determines which two melody cards are the same. When given a correct answer, the teacher plays the named melody on recorder, bells or piano for reenforcing visual-aural learning. This activity is good for a team game with scorekeeping or as an individual-response activity.

Making a People Melody

Ages: 6-8
Equipment: Floor staff
Directions:

One student arranges three other students on the floor staff in a simple melodic order using melody patterns that have been taught. The first student may sing the pattern just arranged, or another student may play/sing it for the first student to approve. Some suggested simple patterns (in treble clef) are:

GE
GGE
GAG
BAG
GAB
GGG

Read and Play

Ages: 6-8
Equipment: Diatonic bells
Five melody patterns on chalk board, each one numbered
Directions:

From a selection of five note patterns on the board, the students challenge each other to play a pattern. This is a good team game with each player, in turn, naming a pattern (Number one, Number two, Number three, etc.) for the opponent to play.

WRITING MELODY

Listening, reading and writing music are an integrated developmental process—all toward the goal of understanding music. Composing and writing original melodies are a part of a child's environment. Young students are skillful in singing and playing original compositions. What fun it is to learn to write these down for other students to perform. Parents and other family members always enjoy them too.

Children must be free to explore and organize sounds for themselves as they discover how to become composers. Repetition of activities is important at this stage. Watch the children carefully during their spontaneous activities. Capture their "personal" songs as you overhear them. Write them into a special composition for everyone to enjoy. The child needs to participate in writing the compositions in order to become a creative musician.

John Holt describes this process by saying, "The only way to get meaning of symbols, to turn other people's symbols into a kind of reality or a mental mode of reality, is by learning first to turn their own reality into symbols. They (the children) have to make the journey from reality to symbol many times before they are ready to go the other way."

Circle Around

Ages: 4-6
Equipment: Large-space manuscript paper
            and pencil for each student
Directions:

Provide the students with pencil and manuscript paper. Have them draw notes on the staff as they sing the verse below.

Verse: (Tune, "Merrily We Roll Along")

Make a circle 'round a line,
'round a line, 'round a line.
Make a circle 'round a line;
Now you have a line note.

Variation: Make space notes by singing, "Make a circle 'round a space . . ."

Melody on a One-Line Staff

Ages: 4-6
Equipment: Prepared chalkboard or work sheet;
                        chalk or pencils
Directions:

Give the students (on work sheet or chalkboard) a one-line staff complete with a G clef (treble clef). Direct the students to write notes above, below, or on the given line. (This results in A, F and G.) Upon completion of this task, the new piece may be performed on any melody instrument. Call these notes by name: F, G, A.

Variation: Students use the same one-line staff to write notes from dictation. The teacher may play the sounds of G, F and A on piano or bells and students write as they hear.

Melody on a Two-Line Staff

Ages: 4-6
Equipment: Prepared chalkboard or work sheet
Directions:

Given a two-line staff (work sheet or chalkboard), the student writes a ten-note melody on the two lines given (Sol and Mi) using whole notes. When the song is completed, it may be performed by teacher and class. Write it on paper and display "Our Composition."

Melodies With Arrows

Ages: 6-8
Equipment: Set of six arrow cards per student or group
                        (3" x 5" cards each with a directional arrow:
                        two cards ascending, 2 descending, 2 horizontal)
Directions:

Given a set of six arrow cards, the student arranges the cards left to right, as he or she wishes the melody to sound. When the cards are arranged to the student's satisfaction, the melody may be performed on bells.

ascending arrow: glissando upwards
descending arrow: glissando downwards
horizontal arrow: repeated tones

Set a Pattern

Ages: 6-8

Equipment: A prepared set of cards: four cards with word "Step" on it; four cards with word "Skip" and four cards with word "Repeat." Music staff on chalkboard or flannel board; chalk or flannel notes.

Directions:

The class is divided into two teams. Team One names the starting note (any note). This note is placed on the staff. Team Two then draws a card from the set. The card indicates whether the next note moves by step, skip or repeat. A player from Team Two places the note in accordance with the card drawn and play passes back to Team One which draws a card and places an appropriate note.

Each correct move earns a team point. The team with the most points is the winner.

Point and Say

Ages: 6-8

Equipment: A music book for each child, chalkboard.

Directions:

As the students look at their music books, a tonal pattern is written on a chalkboard (three notes: any arrangement of repeat, step or skip). It is their task to find a page with the pattern given. The first student to find the named pattern earns a team point or some other special privilege.

Variation: The pattern may be played on the piano or bells.

Match the Note Pattern

Ages: 6-8

Equipment: Set of melody cards
One blank staff card
About eight cardboard notes

Directions:

One melody card is drawn from the set. The student places it in front of him or her. The student also needs one blank staff card and several cardboard notes. The student's job is to place cardboard notes onto the blank staff card so that they will match the pattern given.

After some experience, two students may compete at this activity to see who can finish first.

Variation: This same task may be done with two flannel board staffs; teacher prepares one for student to copy.

Staff to Staff

Ages: 6-8
Equipment: Floor staff and note discs
Flannel board and flannel notes
Directions:

One student places a note pattern on the floor staff. He then calls on another student to place the same pattern on the flannel board. The teacher may play the two patterns on piano or bells to check the move from floor staff to flannel board staff.

For a challenge use this as a team game!

Stepping out a Melody

Ages: 6-8
Equipment: Floor staff
Piano, recorder or bells
Directions:

Standing on the second line of a floor staff (or second space), the student listens carefully while the teacher plays or sings a short, simple melody. The student then steps to places on the staff which correlate to the melody given.

Some suggested patterns:

5	3		
5	3	5	
5	3	5	6
5	6	5	
5	5	3	3

Longer and more complex melodies may be given as students advance in their musical learning.

Hear and Write

Ages: 6-8
Equipment: Piano or recorder for teacher
Paper and pencil for students

Directions:

Students listen to simple tonal patterns on piano or recorder and write what they hear. Have them write letters if you teach syllables; have them write numbers if you teach numbers.

Suggested patterns:

5	3		
5	5	3	
3	5		
3	3	5	
5	3	5	3
3	3	5	3
3	5	1	
1	2	1	
1	3	1	
1	2	3	1

Melody on a Grid: High, Middle, Low

Ages: 6-8
Equipment: Paper grid as pictured (8 1/2" x 11")
5 paper squares as pictures (2 sets of each)

Directions:

Provide a grid marked off High, Middle, Low (referring to pitch placement). Moving left to right along the grid have the student place playing pieces to create a composition. The following playing pieces may be used:

 glissando upward

 glissando downward

 two sounds

 one sound

 three
sounds

Upon completion, the students will have fun playing their own pieces as well as those of classmates on bells or keyboard.

This encourages a "Composer of the Day."

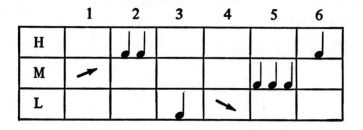

Part Three

GAMES FOR SINGING

Chanting 97
Tone Matching 101
Solo Singing 106
Group Singing 109
Creating Songs 112

Singing is probably the most important musical activity in a young child's musical development. The school day should be filled with spontaneous fun-loving experiences with song. A child remembers these experiences forever, and they help to create enthusiasm for further musical experiences. Singing helps build self-confidence as the child develops from what Piaget calls the "collective monologue" stage into a social being. A child learns to communicate thoughts, to become accepted in a group activity, to expand awareness of self and singing as he or she sings. Sometimes in these early school years it is through music and singing that the child becomes truly happy in the school environment.

CHANTING

Chanting is an important part of the musical development of a child. Through the organization of words verbal understanding is increased and a feeling for rhythm and rhyme is developed.

An important part of a child's social language development comes from creating reality through words and the magical language of imaginary characters. Young children tend to speak aloud with everything from sing-song words to shouts as they accompany movements at play. Before the age of seven, monologues play a major part of their growth patterns. Children often talk and sing to no one in particular. This is part of their thinking and a personal expression of verbal excitement as they learn to take command of the world.

Children love repetition in words, in sounds, or in syllables. Repeated chants are a vital part in the development of language.

A Valentine

Ages: 4-6
Equipment: None
Directions:

The following verse is to be chanted three times: first in a moderate tone, second in a very loud tone, and third in a very soft tone.

Valentine, Valentine, this is true.
Valentine, Valentine, I love you!

The Shopping Center

Ages: 4-6
Equipment: None
Directions:

The children chant in unison and then in groups as directed by the teacher.

(1) Candy, candy, here is a candy store!
Candy, candy, here is a candy store!

(2) Here is a place to eat a steak!
Here is a place to eat a steak!

(3) Let's go to the movies, may we, please?
Let's go to the movies, may we, please?

(4) Shoes! Shoes! I really need new shoes!
Shoes! Shoes! I really need new shoes!

Missing Persons

Ages: 4-6
Equipment: A Nursery Rhyme
Directions:

The class chants a familiar nursery rhyme in unison. The name of the main character is said in a whisper or left out each time it appears.

What a challenge as it trains careful listeners!

Rhyme Dramas

Ages: 4-8
Equipment: Familiar rhymes
Directions:

The teacher directs the class in chanting a familiar rhyme and students are chosen to dramatize the words. Young children love to dramatize nursery rhymes. For more advanced students use a favorite poem or perhaps "Mulberry Street" by Dr. Suess.

Thanksgiving Dinner

Ages: 4-8
Equipment: None
Directions:

The class chants the following in unison, then in groups. Each idea should be spoken in a different tone of voice.

(1) Turkey and dressing! Turkey and dressing!

(2) Cranberry sauce! Cranberry sauce!

(3) Pumpkin pie! Pumpkin pie!

(4) Hot rolls! Hot rolls!

Halloween Night

Ages: 4-8
Equipment: None
Directions:

The class chants the following in unison, then in groups. Each idea should be spoken in a different tone of voice.

(1) Black cats! Black cats!

(2) Skeletons a-dancing! Skeletons a-dancing!

(3) Little yellow pumpkins grinning silly all around!
Little yellow pumpkins grinning silly all around!

Make up your own Halloween story!

Our School

Ages: 4-8
Equipment: None
Directions:

Chant in unison several times as indicated by the teacher. Begin softly; get loud. Begin loudly; get soft. Have fun!

Pencils, tablets, books, books, books!
Pencils, tablets, books, books, books!
Art, math, physical education!
Art, math, physical education!

Language, social studies, recess, lunch!
Language, social studies, recess, lunch!
Music, library, read, read, read!
Music, library, read, read, read!

My Four Voices

Ages: 4-8
Equipment: None
Directions:

Chant in echo fashion—teacher first, students repeat.

I have four voices. (I have four voices.)
This is my speaking voice. (This is my speaking voice.)
This is my shouting voice. (This is my shouting voice.)
This is my whispering voice. (This is my whispering voice.)
(On a tone) This is my singing voice. (This is my singing voice.)

Rhyme Graphing

Ages: 6-8
Equipment: A familiar chant
Directions:

The teacher (or a student) makes a line graph to indicate voice direction. While the graph is traced at the board, the voice must follow the high and low of the graph as a familiar chant is recited.

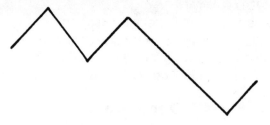

Change a Verse

Ages: 6-8
Equipment: Familiar poems
Directions:

The class discusses different types of voice pitches, tempi, and inflections. A student will then choose how the poem should be chanted. (High/Low; Fast/Slow; Loud/Soft; Gradually Louder/Softer; Short Sounds/Long Sounds, etc.)

A dial to move is fun to use to decide variations.

Nonsense Verses

Ages: 6-8

Equipment: Selected verses
(Nonsense rhymes or limericks)

Directions:

Children love to repeat nonsense verses and selected limericks. Encourage them to create their own and add body sounds.

TONE MATCHING

More teachers have questions concerning how to help children sing in tune than almost any other question. The most important activity is SINGING—singing for fun. A child who has difficulty matching tones should never be embarrassed or singled out of the group. The child should be helped in a variety of ways and always with enthusiasm for the joy of singing.

The most successful interval for tone matching is sol-mi (the descending minor third). This is a "natural" interval which children use in their playground calls.

Some techniques that help students to match pitches are:

* Singing in a small group with stronger singers to feel secure and hear the correct pitch.
* Matching pitches of instruments, particularly the resonator bells. The student can hold these instruments close to the ear.
* Making a variety of sounds to match.
* Linking visual activity to the pitch of the voice—by hand signs on melody direction; by body movement; by melody graphing.
* Performing a variety of breathing exercises for awareness of air passage and lung control.
* Using a variety of voices: speaking, whispering, yelling or singing.
* Keeping the singing experience of tone matching free and without concern for success or failure.

Singing Conversations

Ages: 4-6
Equipment: None
Directions:

The teacher sings the questions and the students sing the replies. This is especially fun on the day after a vacation or a special event.

Suggested questions: (Any questions other than "yes" or "no" questions are best.)

"Where did you go last weekend?"
"Who went with you?"
"What did you do there?"
"What did you have to eat there?"
"Tell me about the weather."
"Was there any trouble?"
"Was there something especially funny?"

Telephone Talk

Ages: 4-6
Equipment: A pair of toy telephones
Directions:

Singing conversations are held by the two who use the telephones. At first it may be teacher and student, with the student being encouraged to sing all conversations on one or two tones (and teacher doing same). Later more freedom may be given to those who "telephone talk" allowing them to sing on any tones so long as the conversation continues to be on a tone. This is a good game to teach telephone manners and listening skills too!

Sing and Spell

Ages: 4-6
Equipment: None
Directions:

The teacher spells the name of a student, using pitches of Sol-Mi. The student echoes the spelling and the pitches. The entire class can echo too.

Variation: A student may sing and spell a friend's name for an echo-response.

Sing Me Your Name

Ages: 4-6
Equipment: Hand drum
Directions:

The teacher sings the name of a student Sol-Mi with a rhythm accompaniment on a hand drum. The student then sings the name back as the teacher accompanies. This is excellent for lining up at the door for dismissal!

SU - SAN   TIM - O - THY

Sirens

Ages: 4-6
Equipment: None
Directions:

The teacher leads the class in speaking and producing appropriate sounds.

Here comes the firetruck with its siren sound.
   Ooh-------------(move hand from low to high as
   corresponding sound is produced)
Here comes the firechief with his new up and down siren.
   Ooh-------------(move hand high to low corresponding
   to sound)

A Hearing Hose

Ages: 4-8
Equipment: A piece of soft plastic hose (about two or three
              feet long) as from a hair dryer or vacuum sweeper.
Directions:

One end of the hose is placed at teacher's mouth and the other end at the student's ear. The student listens carefully as the teacher sings, then places one end of the hose at his mouth and the other end at his ear. The teacher softly sings to the student, who in turn repeats the pattern into the hose, hearing immediately what is produced. This is an excellent way to offer students immediate feedback so far as hearing themselves sing is concerned. It's fun, too!

Humming Together

Ages: 4-8
Equipment: None
Directions:

Place your head next to the young child's head and hum a tone. The child should respond by humming the same tone. This is excellent ear training.

Halloween Night

Ages: 4-8
Equipment: None
Directions:

As the teacher creates a story about Halloween Night the students respond either individually or as a group by making the sounds. For example:

Howling wind
Witches giggling
Ghosts moaning
Cat meowing

For a special activity try dramatizing the story.

Echo Down the Line

Ages: 6-8
Equipment: None
Directions:

The teacher sings a tonal pattern or a phrase from a song to the first student in line. This student sings it and sends it to the next student to sing. The pattern or phrase echoes down the line as long as it has been passed on correctly.

Instrument Pitch

Ages: 6-8
Equipment: Piano or resonator bells
Directions:

The teacher plays a sol-mi pattern on the piano or bells and asks a student to echo the same two pitches back. If the student is correct, he may become the next "pitcher."

This is excellent for some students who can match the sound of an instrument more accurately than they can match another voice.

Same Pitch Call

Ages: 6-8
Equipment: None
Directions:

The teacher sings a student's name with the following chant: "Listen, I am calling, Su-sie." The student echoes her name and can become the next caller.

Variation: One student leaves the room while another hides. When the student reenters the room he is to call for the person he thinks is missing from the class.

Bounce and Hum

Ages: 4-8
Equipment: A small rubber ball
Directions:

Bounce a small rubber ball and with each bounce, hum the tones of "sol-mi." Make the humming so consistent with the bouncing that it becomes a conditioned response. This is excellent for very young children.

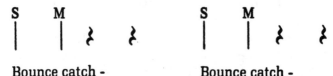

Getting on the Beam

Ages: 4-8
Equipment: A "magic" wand
Directions:

One student is chosen to be "it" and holds the beam (a rhythm stick or baton). Three or four students stand in a line and sing a familiar song. "It" listens to the singing and helps everyone sing in tune. If a student is singing too low, the beam raises higher in the air. If the student is singing too high, the beam lowers to bring the pitch down.

Change the Keys

Ages: 4-8
Equipment: None
Directions:

After the children have learned a simple song, the teacher plays or sings it in several different keys both higher and lower than the original. The children can expand their vocal ranges and enjoy the exploration of sound.

Breathe a Jive

Ages: 4-8
Equipment: A recording of appropriate music
Directions:

As the students hear a "pop" tune, the teacher directs a rhythmic movement to reinforce good breathing habits. For example: taking a big breath, letting breath out slowly, sitting up tall, relaxing shoulders, etc.

SOLO SINGING

Solo singing is an important part of the development of a good singer. Development of self-confidence and stage presence is also an important factor.

It is important to use the correct range of the singing voice and to avoid unrealistic ranges found in some songs. The voice range of an average young singer is from Middle C to the second-space A. As the child matures to eight years old, the range expands to the fifth-line F.

In their early years children enjoy singing independently. They sing easily to a roll call or any type of imitative song. Begin with simple echoing or short responses and as they develop confidence a verse or an entire song can be mastered. Children do not always need an accompaniment. The purity of the young voice is often obscured by the piano. An autoharp or guitar makes a more gentle accompaniment.

Making a tape recording of student performances in class is lots of fun and an excellent way for students to become aware of their own voices. It is fun to share with others on special occasions too!

Who Lives at Your House?

Ages: 4-6
Equipment: None
Directions:

The children sit near the teacher—perhaps in a circle. The teacher pats his or her leg to keep a steady beat and sings on a sol-mi pattern. The children then take turns responding to the questions and singing the answers.

"Who lives at your house?"
"I have a Daddy."
"I have a baby."
"I have a puppy."
"Who lives at your house?"

Puppet Pets

Ages: 4-6
Equipment: Animal puppets
Directions:

Several students are chosen to sing with an animal puppet or marionette. A story can take place in the pet shop or a farmyard or a zoo. The pets are encouraged to create songs as they talk to each other. For a class that needs more direction, try "I Bought Me a Cat" (American Folk Song).

Puppet Play

Ages: 4-6
Equipment: Two or more hand puppets
Directions:

The teacher sings questions for the puppets to answer in a singing voice.

Suggested questions:
"What did you have for lunch?"
"What is your favorite kind of car?"
"Tell me about your favorite movie."

Variation: For additional fun have the puppets sing to each other and tell a story.

Record a Solo

Ages: 4-8
Equipment: Tape recorder
Directions:

Recognize a special child (birthday child; child with exciting news; child who has performed beyond expectations) by allowing the child to hold a microphone and sing into a tape recorder. This activity offers several thrills: holding a microphone, receiving personal attention, and finally listening to the tape. This is a rewarding activity!

Which Song Am I?

Ages: 4-8
Equipment: None
Directions:

A student is chosen to hum or sing "la" on a song of his or her choice. Another student is then chosen to identify the song.

Opera Day

Ages: 4-8
Equipment: None
Directions:

On a specific day both teacher and students sing everything: all directions, questions, answers or conversations. It might be one or two tones or a whole melody.

This is fun for everyone!

Guess Who?

Ages: 6-8
Equipment: None
Directions:

A student is chosen to be "it." "It" turns his back to the class. Another student is chosen to sing a phrase of a song. "It" must then decide who did the singing.

This is a good activity to create independent singers!

Softer Sleuth

Ages: 6-8
Equipment: Blindfold
Directions:

One student is chosen to be blindfolded and another is secretly chosen to be "it." "It" sings a song loudly at first. The blindfolded student walks toward the singing "it." As he or she gets closer to the "it," the song is sung softer and softer. After a correct identification, "it" may become the next sleuth.

Who Can Sing It?

Ages: 6-8
Equipment: None
Directions:

The teacher (or a student) asks, "I am thinking of a song about ..." (which describes a song the class has learned). A student who can guess the song is chosen to sing it for the class.

GROUP SINGING

Group singing is very important. The way to enjoy singing is by singing—singing all types of songs. Children love repetition and become great friends with their favorite songs.

Building a repertoire of familiar songs is always fun for children—not just for school but to take into the home life. Choose songs that are simple, short and with the appropriate voice ranges. Some of the most successful songs are American folk songs that are simple, are easily accompanied, and help to build a valuable repertoire of American heritage.

Other ways to motivate group involvement in singing are through action songs, singing games and singing with props such as puppets or musical dramas. Singing with others is a valuable part of a well-balanced school program.

As students gain the security of lots of singing, they will enjoy singing more and more. Help them to sing all the time, not just at "music time." Music for the young students should be spontaneous—and often!

Hit Parade

Ages: 4-8
Equipment: None
Directions:

Each time children learn a song, write the name on a poster labeled "Hit Parade." Each month sing through the entire repertoire. It is also fun to vote on their "Favorite Song of the Month."

TV Turn-On

Ages: 4-8
Equipment: None
Directions:

The teacher chooses any familiar song and "turns" the group singing on by the movement of the imaginary switch. When the switch turns to "off" the singing must stop. When the switch turns to "on" the singing continues. This is lots of fun and promotes careful listeners!

Missing Words

Ages: 4-8
Equipment: None
Directions:

Choose a familiar song and select important words to leave out. As the group sings the song, a silence takes the place of the missing word.

Try using a picture as a substitute for the word to remind students. This becomes a rebus.

Sing and Go

Ages: 4-8
Equipment: Strips of paper in three colors
Directions:

The students walk around the teacher in a circle while singing a familiar song. The teacher gives strips of different-colored paper to students as she listens to them sing. Colors are determined by (1) in-tune singers, (2) out-of-tune singers, and (3) those undetermined. This is a quick way to evaluate singing ability and have fun at the same time!

Classroom Choir

Ages: 4-8
Equipment: None
Directions:

Students stand and sing like a choir. If risers are available, this is even better. Encourage good posture and performance habits and develop an entire performance repertoire.

Concert Time

Ages: 4-8
Equipment: Good choral recordings
Directions:

Each week should find a time to learn and practice good listening and concert manners. During this time a recording of good choral sound may be played. Children need to hear good singing in order to sing well. Encourage live audience performance manners too!

Performance Please

Ages: 4-8
Equipment: None
Directions:

Encourage individual and small-group student performances in front of the class. This helps to train good audiences while developing self-confidence through performance. Set aside a regular perform-ance time for sharing!

Magic Word Song

Ages: 6-8
Equipment: None
Directions:

A certain word in a song is chosen as a "magic" word. On the "magic" word the entire class will stand or sit down. Choose a song with the "magic" word repeated many times for a lot of fun. For example: "Sing" (Raposo) or "Zip-a-dee doo dah" (Sherman) magic word—zip.

Taped Performance

Ages: 4-8
Equipment: Tape recording
Directions:

From the beginning of the year, keep a taped recording of songs performed in class. This encourages "good" singers and is a good way to show improvement. Students can play the tape for Open House or share with a home-bound student.

Other ideas to promote group singing:

* Use folk songs that tell a story.
  Examples: "Froggie Went a-Courtin' "
* Use musical drama stories.
  Examples: "Little White Duck"
* Use movement while singing.
  Examples: "Three Blind Mice"—3 steps
* Sing unaccompanied and spontaneously and often.
* Use autoharp accompaniment.
* Use rhythm instrument accompaniments.
* Use action songs.
  Examples: "If You're Happy and You Know It"
  "Let Everyone Clap Hands Like Me"
  "Little Peter Rabbit"
  "One Elephant Went Out to Play"
  "Put Your Finger in the Air"
  "Johnny Taps with One Hammer"

CREATING SONGS

Students should be encouraged to compose songs about things that interest them; such as themselves, nature, their family or their friends.

The easiest way to begin creating songs is to take the lead from the students. They are all familiar with "street cries" that you hear them chant on the playground. These are the simple call-response style and can be easily written down. Another easy way to begin is in creating special songs for giving directions. For example: you might have the need to create a song to help pick up the blocks. Using the tune "Looby Loo," sing the words "Let's put the toys away, to use another day!" Children are very adept at creating this type of song.

Encourage them to use a variety of musical expressions, from loud to soft or fast to slow in their songs. Songs should be created to fit their moods. Encourage the young composer by playing and writing music or perhaps taping it for others to listen to. Nothing motivates a young composer better than posting "My Composition" for everyone to see and enjoy!

Shadow Song

Ages: 4-6
Equipment: None
Directions:

One student is chosen as the leader and one as the "echo" or shadow. The leader sings a phrase of his own creation and the shadow repeats the same phrase. The topics can be guided or totally imagined.

This encourages a timid follower to become bolder!

Who Has?

Ages: 4-6
Equipment: None
Directions:

Using the tune to "Mexican Hat Dance" substitute the words: "Who has a new yellow shirt?" (student responds, "I have"). "Who has a pink flowered dress?"

After a few times singing the song, students can create the verses.

Magic Hats

Ages: 4-8
Equipment: A box of costume hats
Directions:

A box that contains hats or simple costumes is a super way to encourage original songs. A student chooses a hat and then sings a

song about the "character" he has become. To encourage the shy
singer try singing with a partner or behind a stage setting.

Mood Music

Ages: 4-8
Equipment: None
Directions:

Explore a range of moods by combining expression and tempo or
created songs to obtain a special feeling. Ask students for a song
about a "happy dog," a sleepy turtle, a sad flower, etc.

For a real challenge try creating the mood through an alphabet
letter or number!

Conversation Opera

Ages: 4-8
Equipment: Box of costumes
Directions:

Set a make-believe stage for the set of a drama. Choose student
volunteers to select a costume and create an action. All of the conversation must be sung as the story is created. Occasional coaching can
encourage a good production.

Improvisation

Ages: 4-8
Equipment: None
Directions:

Occasionally choose a special time for song improvisation.
Choose seasonal topics: "A Mean Old Witch Song," "A Melting
Snowman Song" or current topics: "A Space Shuttle Song" or fun
songs: "A Mouse Who Ate a Tootsiepop," or "The Giant Who Had No
Friends."

Let the students suggest titles to choose from!

Where's My Family?

Ages: 4-8
Equipment: None
Directions:

Students are seated in a circle. The teacher quietly tells each student individually what song to sing. Upon signal each child sings the song he or she has been told to sing. It is the task of the students to group with others who are singing the same song. Try four different songs at first.

Create a Verse

Ages: 4-8
Equipment: None
Directions:

After learning any folk song the students may be encouraged to create other verses. You may wish to use the familiar tune of a folk song and create a new story.

Career Clue

Ages: 6-8
Equipment: None
Directions:

Using this camp song tune, students can sing about different occupations. Tune: "Mary Had a Little Lamb."
For example:
"If I drove a great big truck, great big truck, great big truck, I'll tell you what I'd be . . .
(Spoken) A truck driver I'd be."
"If I helped the sick people, sick people, sick people, I'll tell you what I'd be . . .
(Spoken) A Doctor I'd be."

I Bought Me A . . .

Ages: 6-8
Equipment: None
Directions:

Singing the tune of the American folk song, "I Bought Me a Cat" the student will make substitutions for "cat." For example: "I bought me a *bike* and the *bike* pleased me; I rode my bike to the park and back." Some students will sing in single words and phrases more quickly than entire songs.

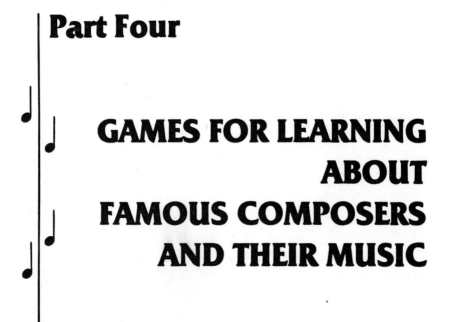

Part Four

GAMES FOR LEARNING ABOUT FAMOUS COMPOSERS AND THEIR MUSIC

The Composers and Their Music 121
   Carnival of the Animals (Saint-Saens) 121
   Danse Macabre (Saint-Saens) 125
   Fantastic Toyshop (Rossini) 127
   Hansel and Gretel (Humperdinck) 128
   March of the Siamese Children (Rodgers) 130
   Minuet (Mozart) 131
   Mother Goose Suite (Ravel) 133
   Nutcracker Suite (Tchaikovsky) 136
   Peer Gynt Suite (Grieg) 139
   Sorcerer's Apprentice (Dukas) 141
   Stars and Stripes Forever (Sousa) 143
Games to Reinforce Knowledge of Literature and Composers ...145

Appreciating music is a personal experience. The greatest gift you can give to your young students is sharing your love and enthusiasm for good music literature.

The secret to presenting a successful listening lesson is the attitude of the teacher. You can help your students become aware of great music literature and famous composers even if you are not familiar with every composition. As you and your students listen repeatedly to a composition, it becomes like an old friend. Children learn very quickly to identify musical themes and are eager to hear them over and over again. Strive to develop a repertoire of familiar music literature that children may feel comfortable with and call their own. You can also encourage children to attend live concerts and share these musical experiences. Many young students listen to good music in their homes and this is a valuable catalyst for many discussions.

Every music literature lesson should have a purpose. Listening is the art of hearing with the mind as well as with the ear. To accomplish this skill, children should be carefully guided in listening for something specific. Children enjoy listening to music that has a story, a captivating rhythm, a singable melody, or that somehow relates to their sphere of interests. At this age, students will be able to identify the story, a specific instrument, the mood, the composer, and perhaps a main theme. It is necessary to challenge their creative imaginations along the line of mood, or what the music is saying to them. However, care must be taken that information about a selection is always secondary to the enjoyment of the music. It is possible to allow a collection of facts to overpower the true essence of a composition. On occasion, a "quiet time" listening is equally important. This might involve a trip in guided imagery or be purely for total relaxation during which music is played.

It is wise to begin helping students to "actively" listen by presenting music that tells a story. As the habit of actively listening is established through the use of compositions that stimulate the imagination, children may be led to an intelligent understanding and enjoyment of great music literature. Only through this gradual process in personal discovery of what the music says to them will young students honestly remember and treasure it.

Have fun with music literature selections by doing any or all of the following:

1. Present the story of the music (or the composer) and then play some of the music.
2. Create a mood in preparation for listening to the music.
3. Listen for specific things (sounds, instruments, main themes).
4. Create original words to sing to the main theme to help recognize it again.
5. Listen to the music first, and then discuss what the story might be.
6. Dramatize the form of a composition (use hats or costumes).
7. Dramatize the movement of a composition (tempo changes, dynamics or mood).
8. Dramatize the rhythm of the composition. (March or waltz).
9. Create hand or body movements to reinforce the rhythm pattern.
10. Pretend to be a composer by creating an original song from a picture or a story.
11. Post a "Hit Parade" of favorite compositions.
12. Keep props handy in a special box (hats, scarves, costumes, etc.).

Listen to lots of music in the classroom to share the simple enjoyment of good music all day long!

All selections of music literature chosen for this chapter are available from the Bowmar/Noble Orchestral Library - Series I.

Bowmar/Noble Music Publishers, Inc.
4563 Colorado Boulevard
Los Angeles, California 90039

THE COMPOSERS AND THEIR MUSIC

The Carnival of the Animals

composed by
Camille Saint-Saens
France
(1835 - 1921)

Composer

Once there was a man named Camille Saint-Saens. He lived in France many years ago. He loved animals; he had many friends; and he loved music.

One day Mr. Saint-Saens decided to write a musical story that would tell about a "carnival of animals." He decided that he would put lots of animals in it, that some of them would be real animals, and that some of them would just be a silly idea. He had a lot of fun writing "The Carnival of the Animals" and when it was done he shared it with his friends. They liked it a lot because some parts of it made them laugh and laugh. Other parts made them think beautiful thoughts.

People today still enjoy hearing "The Carnival of the Animals."

Story

Once upon a time there was a wonderful parade. It was a parade that was fun, colorful, and different from any other parade because it was a parade of animals. The animals organized it; they planned it; and they performed in it.

The animals decided that their parade would be led by the "King of the Jungle," which was the lion. He liked to make a big roar. They told the lion to lead their parade like a good king should and to roar every once in a while to let everyone know he was the king. And he did.

Royal March of the Lion Theme:

Many kinds of animals were in the parade. First were a flock of hens and chickens. They were very busy gossiping together, "cut-cut-cut-cut-cut-cut-ca-da-cut." They said it over and over again.

Hens and Cocks Theme:

Here comes a wild donkey! Just see his energy and joy! This wild donkey really loves the parade.

Next comes a very slow-moving creature. In fact, this is the slowest moving creature in the whole parade! All the other animals come along slowly behind. Even the slow movers have fun in the parade. Here comes the pokey turtle.

Turtle Theme:

What a funny sight the next one is! The big fat elephant is so happy to be in the parade that she is dancing a graceful waltz. Did you ever see such a funny sight as an elephant doing a waltz?

Elephant Theme:

A kangaroo is an animal that moves by jumping. Listen closely to the kangaroo's part in this parade. You will hear jumping music and perhaps you can imagine the kangaroo jumping too. Can you jump like a kangaroo?

Kangaroo Theme:

Here is a great big tank filled with beautiful fish. The water is rippling gently in the tank; the water looks blue and cool. The fish are gold and green and red and yellow. They love to swim and dart about inside their tank. They are especially glad to be in a parade. They love the parade!

Aquarium Theme:

Here comes that wild donkey again! He makes his long ears stand up high and he kicks his heels at sudden stops. Do you think the other animals like to have this wild donkey in their parade?

Around the corner comes a beautiful float. My, what a lot of work went into this part of the parade! There are trees, trees, trees, so many trees of every kind. Tall ones, short ones, big ones, small ones, and bushes all around. I wonder what animal is in that deep forest. It must be very small and hard to find. I cannot see any kind of animal anywhere. Wait! I heard something. What is it? Oh, a bird! A small bird in a tree. It flies around, now and then stopping to sing its same song.

Why, this is a cuckoo bird. It is so happy to be in the parade!

Cuckoo in the Deep Woods Theme:

Just look at that enormous birdcage! I have never seen such a sight! It's no wonder that they had to put this giant birdcage on the back of a big truck. This birdcage is so large that the birds probably think they are out of doors. It has flowers and vines and trees and everything in it. And birds of every color. They play about so freely. They sing and play and make a beautiful sight for the parade!

What is this? I thought it was an animal parade and here come two piano players! Why, they are not animals at all. Their music sounds like scales. It doesn't even sound like a real tune. Well, I say if those piano players can play only scales, they do belong in a zoo. Let's leave them right here in the animal parade where they belong. Silly piano players!

How did bones and fossils get into this parade? They're not animals!

Fossils Theme:

It looks as if they saved the loveliest part until now. Did you ever see such a pretty pool of smooth clear water? And did you ever see such a beautiful white swan? Notice how gracefully and smoothly the swan glides through the water. This quiet animal helps me to feel quiet and calm, too. The swan loves to be in the parade.

Swan Theme:

Let's take one more quick look at all the animals. Which ones can you see again? I wonder if those wild donkeys will come this way again.

Finale Theme:

I am so happy that the animals made a parade. And I'm glad that we got to be there, Aren't you?

Activities:

1. Stage your own parade. Assign various children to "act out" the respective animals as they appear in the music.

2. Make a mural. Provide paper and crayons for the class to illustrate a parade of animals. Display the mural in the school hallway.

3. Make a booklet. Present "The Carnival of the Animals" over a period of several days with the children preparing one booklet page each day. The pages may contain musical examples as well as illustrations. Assemble the pages into a completed book for keeping.

4. Excerpt some favorite parts to be repeated occasionally in future days. "The Swan" is useful for creating quiet in the classroom; the introduction is useful as an energizer on a lazy day; "The Aquarium" is useful for free creative movement, etc.

5. Make the record available in a listening center so that students may hear it as desired.

Danse Macabre

composed by
Camille Saint-Saens
France
(1835 - 1921)

Composer

Camille Saint-Saens began noticing musical sounds at the age of two. His mother, an artist, encouraged the young Saint-Saens' talent. At the age of six, he gave his first concert. He became a brilliant pianist and composer. He was well loved in his native France and enjoyed reading and traveling.

Story

On a frosty autumn night, many long years ago a strange thing happened in a graveyard. It was Halloween night and the frost-bitten leaves were scurrying across the tombstones.

Just as the clock in the village tower struck midnight a ghostly figure appeared in the graveyard carrying a fiddle under his chin. The figure was Old Death who for many years appeared only on Halloween night to play for a party in honor of the ghosts on Halloween. As he passed by each gravestone, the skeletons came to life. Their bones creaked as they danced over the graveyard.

The happy ghosts skipped and danced over the dry leaves as their bones crackled and crunched.

They were having a wonderful time at their yearly party when suddenly dawn began to lighten the sky. Just then the terrifying sound of the cock crowing rang out in the cool air. Silence fell immediately and all the skeletons scurried into the ground. The dawn of a new day had arrived.

Activities

1. Dramatize the story.
2. Listen for Death to tune his fiddle; for the skeletons to dance; for the cock to crow.
3. Play rhythm instruments along with the skeleton dance.
4. Create your own drama for Halloween.
5. Listen to the music first and see if you can tell what the musical story is all about.

The Fantastic Toyshop

composed by
Gioacchino Rossini
Italy
(1792 - 1868)

Composer

Rossini was born into a family of traveling musicians. He began singing solos as a young boy and at the age of fourteen composed his first opera. He liked to play jokes on people to make them laugh. As Rossini became older he wrote many famous operas, which his audiences always enjoyed.

About fifty years after the death of Rossini, a composer named Respighi arranged one of Rossini's musical pieces into an orchestral ballet suite. It was called "The Fantastic Toyshop."

Story

Once upon a time there was a toyshop run by a shopkeeper and his young helper. Many people visited the shop to see the mechanical dolls. Two special families came to the shop very often. Unfortunately, both families wanted to buy the same two Italian dolls. These Italian dolls danced the "Tarantella."

Tarantella Theme:

Each family decided to buy one doll. They happily paid for the dolls and decided to return for them the next day. All the dolls were put away and the shop closed for the night.

At the stroke of midnight the dolls magically came to life and had a big party. The other dolls became worried about the Italian dolls leaving the shop. They decided to hide them for protection.

The next morning when the shop opened, the families came to get their dolls. The boxes were handed to them. They lifted the lids and found—nothing. The families became furious and the dolls suddenly came to life and started chasing the people away. Later in the day the families peered through the shop window. Imagine their surprise when they saw the dolls dancing around the shopkeeper.

Activities

1. Listen to other selections from "The Fantastic Toyshop"
2. Recreate the drama of the story.
3. Create a dance to the music.
4. Create your own toyshop story.
5. Listen to the music before hearing the story to discover the musical story.

Hansel and Gretel

composed by
Englebert Humperdinck
Germany
(1854 - 1921)

Composer

Humperdinck grew up in Germany in a happy family. He and his sister, Adelheid, enjoyed playing together and especially enjoyed acting out fairy tales. Adelheid made up the stories and Engelbert created the songs. Although later in life he studied to become an architect, Humperdinck turned to music and became very famous. Even today outside his family home in Germany are little statues of Hansel and Gretel, for which he had become so famous.

Story

The "Overture" to Hansel and Gretel sets the mood as it introduces the listener to melodies that follow in the opera.

Once upon a time in a poor cottage in Germany lived a broom-maker and his wife. They had two children, Hansel and Gretel. One day, after eating the last crumb of bread in the house, the mother and father set out to sell the brooms they had made. Hansel and Gretel worked at their chores for a while but became bored and began to dance and play.

Upon returning home, the mother noticed that the chores were not completed as she had asked. She became angry and sent the children into the forest to pick berries.

The children picked berries, resting occasionally and eating some berries. Suddenly it became dark and the children, not used to spending the night alone in the woods, became very frightened. The children said their prayers and the Sandman helped them to go to sleep while fourteen angels descended from heaven to guard them.

Prayer Theme:

At dawn they were awakened by the Dew Fairy.

Dew Fairy Theme:

They began walking again and suddenly, much to their surprise, they saw a little house made of cakes and candy with a gingerbread fence surrounding it. They ran toward the house and began to nibble on the cakes when suddenly a squeaky voice came from inside. "Nibble, nibble, mouse-kin, who's nibbling at my house-kin?" The children were surprised to see the door of the little house open and an ugly old witch peer from the door.

Witch's Theme:

She caught Hansel and trapped him in a cage. She had plans to fatten him up and eat him. The witch ordered Gretel to look in the oven to see if the gingerbread was ready. Gretel pretended not to understand. When the old witch opened the oven to show Gretel how to test the gingerbread, Gretel gave her an enormous shove. Into the oven the old witch went.

In a twinkling, the house disappeared and in place of the gingerbread fence were a row of children. The magic spell was broken. Everyone danced with joy because they were rescued from the terrible witch. The children all returned home and lived happily ever after.

Rescue Theme:

Activities

1. Dramatize the story.
2. Identify the main themes by listening to the music.
3. Discover other songs from the opera.
4. Create your own opera.
5. Illustrate scenes from the opera.

March of the Siamese Children

"The King and I"
Composed by
Richard Rodgers
United States of America
(1902 - 1979)

Composer

Once there was a man named Richard Rodgers who loved to write musical stories. He wrote his stories so that they were performed like plays on a stage. There was always music and singing by everyone in the story. Richard Rodgers became very famous for the musical plays that he wrote. Every year for many years he wrote a new musical play. One of his musical plays was called "The King and I."

Story

Once upon a time there was a great teacher named Anna who went to teach the King's children in a country called Siam. The King had many children and he and his helpers told the children that their new teacher, Anna, would be coming soon. The children were told that when Anna arrived they should line up outside and enter in a single file to parade before Anna. They practiced walking carefully, stopping in front of Anna, and giving a deep, low bow. The Siamese children practiced this greeting for Anna many times and they grew quite impatient waiting for her to arrive.

Finally the day came when Anna did arrive in Siam. The children were so happy that their teacher had arrived at last. They put on their finest clothing and excitedly lined up outside the door to go in and greet their new teacher just as they had practiced. Some of the children were very small; others were quite big. Some were very shy and others were rowdy and noisy. The King of Siam sat on a big chair with Anna beside him.

The King said, "Miss Anna, here are my children. These are the Siamese children." The children entered one by one to greet their new teacher.

Activities

1. Dramatize the story of the music.
2. Accompany the music with percussion instruments (drums, gongs, woodblocks, triangles, or finger cymbals).
3. Clap the rhythm pattern softly as it occurs in the music.

        | ⌐⌐ | ⌐⌐

4. Illustrate the rondo form (ABACABA) of the music to make an interesting study in contrast and repetition as well as an attractive illustration.

Minuet

Composed by
Wolfgang Amadeus Mozart
Austria
(1756 - 1791)

Composer

Wolfgang Amadeus Mozart was one of the most famous composers of all time. Mozart was born into a musical family and listened to much music in his childhood. When he was four years old, his father taught him to play little minuets and other dances. When he was five years old he composed his first minuet. While still very young, Mozart traveled all over Europe performing for Kings and Queens. At the age of eight, he wrote his first symphony. Mozart has given the world much happiness with his many famous compositions.

Story

Once upon a time when Wolfgang Amadeus Mozart was about six years old, he and his sister, Nannerl, were playing games together at the clavier. (A clavier was the type of keyboard instrument which people had in the olden days before the piano was invented.) Amadeus and Nannerl loved to play together and they both especially loved to play games that included music. On this particular day, Nannerl, who was a little older than Amadeus, would play a short tune on the clavier while Amadeus covered his eyes; then Amadeus would try to play the same tune. He was very good at the game and Nannerl would clap and cheer for him every time. After a while Amadeus said, "Nannerl, it's my turn to play on the clavier for you to repeat after me. Here now, close your eyes." Nannerl closed her eyes tightly. She even put her hands over them to be very fair with her little brother. Amadeus went to the clavier and began to play a new minuet that Nannerl had never heard before. After the first phrase, Nannerl opened her eyes and was about to go to the clavier; but her brother kept on playing. He played phrase after phrase and he seemed to have forgotten all about the game. Nannerl sat listening quietly. She thought her brother's minuet was lovely. She was so proud of him for making such beautiful music! Finally, the music came to an end. Nannerl clapped and clapped. "Oh, Amadeus," she said. "Will you please play your minuet again so that I can dance?" And he did.

A minuet is a dance in little steps. In the time of George Washington the minuet was a very popular dance.

Minuet Themes:

Activities

1. Learn to dance the minuet.
2. Listen to other compositions by Mozart.
3. Pretend to be attending a concert in the court of the King while you listen to the minuet.
4. Discuss how dances in the days of Mozart are different from dances of today.

Mother Goose Suite

Composed by
Maurice Ravel
France
(1875 - 1937)

Composer

Maurice Ravel grew up in a musical family and he was always interested in becoming a musician. When he was very young, his father encouraged him to play the piano. Sometimes his father even paid the young Ravel to practice his piano lessons. At the age of twelve, Ravel started studying composition seriously. He won many awards for his musical compositions. Ravel had a sense of humor and loved to play practical jokes on his friends.

Ravel's music became very famous for the unusual instrumental sounds and vivid rhythmic effects. He was one of the French impressionistic composers.

Story

Ravel wrote "The Mother Goose Suite" especially for young children. "The Mother Goose Suite" is a series of five pieces, each telling the story of a favorite fairy tale to music. The pieces are: Sleeping Beauty, Hop O'My Thumb, Laideronette, Beauty and the Beast, and The Fairy Garden.

I. THE SLEEPING BEAUTY

Once upon a time, in a kingdom long ago, two beautiful princesses were born. At the christening, twelve good fairies were invited to present gifts, but unfortunately, one bad fairy also came. In her fury she cast a spell on one of the princesses saying, "I endow you with perfect ugliness." And in a flash of lightning, the bad fairy had disappeared.

The Queen grabbed her little princess and the other fairies gathered around. Each minute the little girl grew uglier and uglier. The good fairies promised happiness in spite of the ugliness. The two baby princesses fell asleep under the spell of the wicked fairy. The good fairies danced slowly around them to the music of a pavane.

Pavane of the Sleeping Beauty Theme:

II. HOP O' MY THUMB

Years later, the Ugly Princess, Laideronette, went to live in a castle far away on the other side of a dense forest. In the forest lived Hop O' My Thumb, who with his seven brothers was spreading crumbs so that they would be able to find their way back home. Unfortunately the birds ate the crumbs and the boys tried and tried to find their way as they searched for the right path.

Hop O' My Thumb Theme:

III. LAIDERONETTE

The Ugly Princess, Laideronette, met a huge green snake during her walk through the forest. The snake told her, "Don't feel bad little princess; I am uglier than you." The snake took the Ugly Princess to his palace in the land of the Pagoda people. He then changed into a handsome prince and Laideronette changed into a beautiful princess. She lived happily ever after as Empress of the Pagodas.

Laideronette Theme:

IV. BEAUTY AND THE BEAST

Meanwhile, the beautiful princess met an ugly Beast who had a deep grumbling voice. She was very afraid but tried to be brave. Before long, she realized that the Beast was very kind. She promised to marry him. At that very moment, the Beast was transformed into a handsome prince.

Princess Theme:

Beast Theme:

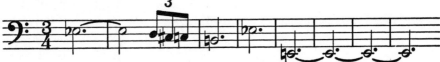

V. THE FAIRY GARDEN

"The Fairy Garden" tells the story of Sleeping Beauty awakening from her long sleep. All of the people in the palace awaken and even the flowers join in a dance in the garden. The entire court once again becomes joyful.

Dance Theme:

Activities

1. Discuss Mother Goose stories that are familiar rhymes.
2. Tell the fairy tales that Ravel uses in his Suite.
3. Play "The Sleeping Beauty" by Tchaikovsky.
4. Dramatize the story as it is told or played.
5. Enjoy the music for quiet listening.

Nutcracker Suite

Composed by
Peter Tchaikovsky
Russia
(1840 - 1893)

Composer

Peter Tchaikovsky loved music very much as a little boy. He began piano lessons when he was five years old. When he was young he began using his vivid imagination to compose many pieces. Tchaikovsky studied to become a lawyer but never really enjoyed it. He returned to his real love—music.

Story

The "Nutcracker Suite" is a ballet based on a fairy tale of the magic in a family Christmas celebration.

It was Christmas Eve and a little girl, named Marie, was having a family party. Marie received a Nutcracker from her uncle. It was her favorite present. Her brother, Fritz, wanted to see the Nutcracker and grabbed for it, only to break the toe. Marie was so unhappy. She cried as she rocked the Nutcracker to sleep in a doll cradle. Then she went to bed.

In the middle of the night, Marie woke up and tiptoed downstairs to see if her Nutcracker felt better. She was amazed to see the tree lights on and the toys marching about the room. Leading the parade was the Nutcracker.

March Theme

Suddenly an army of mice attacked the soldiers and a terrible battle began. Marie jumped into the battle and threw her shoe at the Mouse King, stopping the battle.

The Nutcracker magically came to life and invited Marie on a journey to "The Land of the Sugar Plum Fairy." While in this land, Marie saw many dolls dancing.

She saw the Sugarplum Fairy dancing very daintily to some high delicate music.

Sugarplum Fairy Theme:

Next came the Russian dancers doing a very fast dance, the Trepak.

Trepak Theme:

In the Arabian Dance, Marie could clearly hear the desert winds blowing very gently. The dance seemed strangely mysterious to Marie.

Arabian Dance Theme:

The Chinese Dance made Marie laugh and laugh. She loved to watch the short shuffling steps as she listened to the music.

Chinese Dance Theme:

No sooner had the Chinese dancers finished than three toy flutes came to life and began to dance. Their dance ws lively as they played this merry tune.

Dance of the Flute Theme:

Just before it was time to leave, Marie heard some beautiful harp music. The flowers had all come to life and were dancing a waltz just for Marie.

Waltz of the Flowers Theme:

As if by magic, Marie opened her eyes and found that she was in her own bed. The moonlight was pouring in through her bedroom windows creating a mystical glow in the room. She was no longer in the Land of the Sugarplum Fairy, but in her own soft white bed at home. It had been a wonderful dream.

Activities

1. Dramatize the story as it is told or played.
2. Create other events in the Land of the Sugarplum Fairy.
3. Use rhythm instruments to accompany the music.
4. Dance to the music.
5. Identify the instruments used in the different parts of the Ballet.
6. Identify the country represented by the Trepak (Russia) or the Chinese Dolls (China).
7. Discuss what makes a ballet.

In the Hall of the Mountain King

"Peer Gynt Suite"
Composed by
Edvard Grieg
Norway
(1843 - 1907)

Composer

Many years ago there lived in Norway a young man named Edvard Grieg. He loved his country very deeply. He loved the mountains, the lakes, the hills and the flowers. He thought that his country was the most wonderful country on earth! He loved the stories of his country—the old fairy tales and legends. He thought the stories were interesting to hear and fun to know. The stories that he especially liked were about a rascal named Peer Gynt. Peer, even as a little boy, was forever making trouble for himself and others. He seemed to find trouble wherever he went. Mr. Grieg was not a troublemaker, but he did love to hear about Peer Gynt. Mr. Grieg loved to write music and so he decided to take the fairy tales of Peer Gynt and write them into music.

Story

One day when Peer Gynt was out looking for an adventure he wandered into a cave. It was a dark cave in the side of a big mountain. He knew he should not be there, but he went anyway. As he roamed around inside the cave, he suddenly stumbled into a large cave room filled with very small troll people. He knew that he was in the Hall of the Mountain King.

Hall of the Mountain King Theme:

The trolls welcomed him kindly. Peer returned the greeting by telling the trolls what a wonderful fellow he was, how smart and clever and powerful. The trolls were very impressed! They decided that Peer Gynt should marry their princess and they arranged it immediately.

Peer Gynt did not want to marry the troll king's daughter. He did not want to have anything to do with these troll people. He told the trolls that he would not marry the princess and he started to leave. The trolls were very angry now and would not let Peer leave. They made a large circle around him and began to torment him with angry words. As they continued to think what a rascal he was, they began to poke him and jab him, moving the circle closer and closer to him. Peer Gynt was feeling quite frightened and was very thankful when, in the end, he was able to make his escape.

Activities

1. Create a dance to the music.
2. Dramatize the story. Listen to the music and move about as the mountain trolls might have done (beginning slowly and

gaining movement and excitement in accordance with the music.)

3. Create a rhythmic drawing. Use crayons to make marks that agree with the rhythms.
4. Discuss Peer Gynt. What sort of fellow was he? What did he do to get into this troublesome situation? What might he have done differently?
5. Use the music for a Halloween frolic.

Sorcerer's Apprentice

Composed by
Paul Dukas
France
(1865 - 1935)

Composer

Once there was a man named Paul Dukas. He lived in France many years ago. One day he heard a wonderful, exciting story named "The Sorcerer's Apprentice." Mr. Dukas liked the story so much that he decided to retell the story in music. He decided that his music would be played by an orchestra, that it would contain no talking or singing, and that the instruments of the orchestra would simply tell the story.

Story

Once upon a time there was a little boy named Romanoff. He wanted to learn to be a great Sorcerer. So he enrolled to take lessons with a famous Sorcerer who lived nearby. Romanoff went to the Master's house every day and there he had daily lessons on how to become a great Sorcerer. Romanoff was a student or Apprentice.

One day the Master Sorcerer went away and left Romanoff in charge of things. The Master left Romanoff a list of things to do. One of the tasks was to fill the Master's bathtub with water from the well. Romanoff obediently began to bring in the water from the well. Then he began to think. He thought, "Why should I be doing this hard work when I could be having it done by magic? It is true that I have had only a few lessons in sorcery, but commanding a broom to carry water was the very first thing that I learned. I think I will do that now. Then the broom can carry all this heavy water and I can rest." So he did.

Romanoff sat down and began to think very hard. He thought of magic powers; he thought magical thoughts.

Magic Powers Theme:

He called out some magic words and the broom slowly began to carry out Romanoff's command. The broom's steps were slow and hesitant at first and gradually became faster and faster

Broom Theme:

The broom became more and more enthusiastic, bringing more and more water. It moved faster and faster. Soon the bathtub filled with water and the lazy Romanoff realized that he didn't know how to get the broom to stop. He had not been taught that part of the magic lesson! Poor Romanoff. He tried everything: yelling "Stop," shouting magic words, chopping the broomstick into bits. Nothing worked and the water continued to rise in the bathtub. Soon water was running over the top of the tub and into the house.

The Master Sorcerer arrived home. He pronounced the proper magic words and order was restored.

Activities

1. Have children take turns relating the story of the Apprentice.
2. Dramatize the story with special actors assigned as the Master, the Apprentice, the First Broom, the Other Brooms.
3. Illustrate favorite parts of the story.

4. Clap softly during the Broom Theme and listen quietly during the other parts.

The Stars and Stripes Forever

Composed by
John Philip Sousa
United States of America
(1854 - 1932)

Composer

Once there was a young boy named John Philip Sousa whose father was a member of the United States Marines. When John Philip was growing up in Washington D.C., his father took him to many band rehearsals and concerts. John Philip even learned to play several musical instruments. He loved to watch his father play in the Marine Band and he often wished that someday he could be a band director.

When John Philip grew up, his wish came true. He not only became a band director; he even got the job of directing the United States Marine Band! He was very glad that his wish had come true.

John Philip Sousa loved his band; he loved the Marines; and he loved the United States of America. He discovered that he also liked to write music for his band to play. His favorite compositions were marches which seemed to have a wonderful spirit of love for his country and his band. Many of his marches are still played today. Some people call him the "March King" because he wrote so many marches. One of his most famous is called "The Stars and Stripes Forever."

Story

Have you looked at the flag of the United States and seen the stars? Have you noticed the stripes? John Philip Sousa noticed them. He loved that flag with the stars and stripes and told his friends that he hoped it would wave forever as a symbol of the United States. He felt so strongly about it that he wrote a special march. He titled it, "The Stars and Stripes Forever."

The first theme seems to say, "Hey, look at this great nation which I represent!"

First Theme:

The second theme seems to say, "This nation is so strong that it will always be great!"

Second Theme:

John Philip Sousa's music made everyone want to march proudly and say, "Hurrah for the flag of the free!"

Activities:

1. Play rhythm instruments along with the record. Assign different instruments to play during different sections.
2. March around the room to the music. Try a single file as you march through zig-zag patterns, concentric circles and square corners.
3. Illustrate the United States flag. Display it with a story about John Philip Sousa.
4. Assign two groups of students to march in place. One group will march on Theme One and the other group will march on Theme Two.
5. Use flannelgraph materials to illustrate the form of this march (Intro A A B B C C Bridge C C). Symbols such as stars, stripes or flags or even alphabet letters may be used.

GAMES TO REINFORCE KNOWLEDGE OF LITERATURE AND COMPOSERS

Match Mine

Ages: 4-6
Equipment: A length of yarn
Prepared pictures representing several familiar compositions
Directions:

As students listen to a familiar musical composition, several pictures representing the compositions are displayed in the front of the room. Students take turns making a circle of the yarn around the picture that matches the music they hear.

Which One Do You Hear?

Ages: 4-8
Equipment: Three prepared pictures representing literature selections
Directions:

Three pictures representing specific literature are displayed for the students. As the literature selection is played, the students determine which piece of music they hear. The student with the correct answer can choose the next selection.

Treasure Hunt

Ages: 4-8
Equipment: Pictures representing music literature selections
Directions:

Pictures of several music literature selections are displayed in odd places around the room. It is the task of the student to discover the correct picture when the recording of the selection is played.

Variation: A discussion of the picture can replace the playing of the selection.

Which Am I?

Ages: 4-8
Equipment: Recordings of appropriate music
Directions:

After the students are familiar with the sound of a *choir*, a *band*, or an *orchestra*, play a specific selection. It is their task to determine which type of group is performing.

Musical Collage

Ages: 4-8
Equipment: Pictures of music performers or groups
Directions:

Students are requested to bring pictures from magazines or newspapers in categories of Band, Ballet, Orchestra, Choir, etc. The pictures are glued onto a collage for everyone to enjoy.

How Can I Compose This?

Ages: 4-8
Equipment: Story ideas
Directions:

The students are presented a situation or a story. They are to become composers. It is their task to determine, "If I were the composer how would I write this music?" They can decide: "Would it be a band?" "Would it be a ballet?" "Would it be a choir?" "Would it be fast or slow?" "Would it be loud or soft?" etc.

Variation: How can I write a song to describe a turtle? A rabbit?

Composer Count

Ages: 6-8
Equipment: Newspaper or media reports
Directions:

Students are requested to listen to the television/radio news or have their parents help them watch for activities in the local area which relate to music or composers. Make a bulletin board of clippings.

Composer Train

Ages: 6-8
Equipment: About ten chairs set in double rows
Directions:

The teacher reads a descriptive fact concerning a composer. The student correctly identifying the composer earns a trip on the train-of-composers.

Variation: Students may also identify a specific composition to ride the train.

How Many?

Ages: 6-8
Equipment: None
Directions:

Students are requested to count how many radios, televisions, stereo components, etc., they have in their homes. A graph or listing can be made in the classroom to compile data. Discussion can cover listening to music and perhaps keeping a record of types of music played in the home.

About Town

Ages: 6-8
Equipment: None
Directions:

Students are requested to bring to class any programs or comments on concerts or music events in their community. A bulletin board is prepared to collect the shared items.

Who Is The Composer?

Ages: 6-8
Equipment: Recordings of appropriate music
Directions:

As the students listen to a short music selection they have studied, it is their task to determine who the composer is. They might indicate their choice by telling something they remember about the composer, speak his name, or show his picture.

Who Am I?

Ages: 6-8
Equipment: None
Directions:

A student is selected to describe a composer studied. It is the task of the class to decide which composer it is. A cumulative composer bulletin board would be helpful here.

Three Square

Ages: 6-8
Equipment: Paper and crayons or pencils
Directions:

Prepare for each student a sheet of paper with a tic-tac-toe grid. In each square the student draws a picture to represent the familiar literature selection as requested. Nine titles will be needed to completely fill in the grid. Students may enter each title in any random-choice space. When the title of the music is played, the student covers the square to indicate that he has identified the selection. The student who is first to cover three squares in a row is the winner.

Variation: Have papers prepared in advance. For a more difficult game each card would be different!

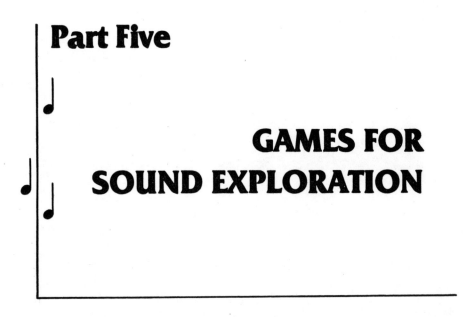

Part Five

GAMES FOR SOUND EXPLORATION

Ideas for Producing Sounds 151
Making Instruments 163

Washboards　　　　　Pasta
Bottle caps　　　　　Seeds
Paper clips　　　　　Buttons
Grains
Rattling Sounds
Gravel　　　　　　　*Plus:*
Stones　　　　　　　Brushes, rubber bands,
Dried pods　　　　　balloons and hoses

Sound Match

Ages: 4-6
Equipment: A Feely Box filled with such things
as two small sticks, two small rattles,
two scraps of sandpaper, two dried pods, etc.
Directions:

One student is chosen as "it." His task is to reach inside the Feely Box and select two matching sound objects. If his match is correct, he may choose the next player. To test a correct match, try playing them rather than just looking at them.

Find My Sound

Ages: 4-6
Equipment: A Feely Box filled with such sound producers
as a rattle, a whistle, a brush, a rubber band,
crumbled paper, etc.
Directions:

One student is chosen as "it." He listens to the hidden sound of an object which has a match in the Feely Box. It is his task to select the same object from the Box that he heard. A correct response entitles "it" to produce the next sound.

Animal Sounds

Ages: 4-6
Equipment: None
Directions:

The teacher uses a simple chant to encourage students to use various voice qualitites in making animal sounds:

Verse:

"Randy is a tiger, a tiger, a tiger.
Randy is a tiger, listen to him growl."
"Susan is a dog, a dog, a dog.
Susan is a dog, listen to her bark."

High And Low Sounds

Ages: 4-6
Equipment: Piano or resonator bells
Directions:

Students listen as the teacher plays a single tone on the piano. When they hear a high sound, they should reach up very high. When they hear a low sound, they bend to the ground.

Where Am I?

Ages: 4-6
Equipment: None
Directions:

All players hide their eyes. The teacher tiptoes to some spot in the room and makes a sound (hand clap, bell, etc.). The teacher then tiptoes away from that spot and announces, "Ready," The players must tell where the teacher was when the sound was made. They may also want to identify the sound.

Sound Signals

Ages: 4-6
Equipment: Any sound-producing materials
Directions:

The teacher selects a sound and designates a special meaning for it. One sound will mean "listen," another "sit down," or another "come to the circle." Each time the sound is produced the students respond. These cues are good to use all year!

How Many?

Ages: 4-6
Equipment: None
Directions:

The students name as many things as they can think of that make a sound. As they are named, the teacher will write them on the board.

Variation: Things at home that make a sound? Things at school that make a sound? Things at the park that make a sound?

How Many Got Caught?

Ages: 4-6
Equipment: Sound-producing objects
Directions:

One student ("It") is directed to shut his or her eyes. The teacher improvises a story, which may have one, two, or three students playing instruments. For example: "Once upon a time there was a family of mice. They were hungry and went out to find some cheese. The sly old cat was listening to them. Can you tell how many he caught?" The number caught is determined by how many students are playing. "It" tries to tell the correct answer.

Sound Walk

Ages: 4-6
Equipment: None
Directions:

The teacher guides the students on a Sound Walk using creative imagery. The pretend walk will involve student creation of sounds as the teacher tells a story. One successful way to encourage individual participation is to go around the circle as each student in turn gives a sound.

The sounds might include: walking noises, a car, a bike, a skateboard, the wind, the birds, a dog, etc.

Gerbil Music

Ages: 4-6
Equipment: Sound-producing objects
Directions:

The students explore sounds to discover what might sound appropriate to tell about the life of a gerbil. This is good for discussion and students can then create a sound composition. Perhaps it can be written down for a classroom performance.

Where's the Sound?

Ages: 4-6
Equipment: A variety of sound-producing objects
Directions:

"It" stands with his back to the performer. As the performer plays the sound (above the head; to the right; to the left) it is the task of "it" to point in the direction of the sound.

By Chance

Ages: 6-8
Equipment: None
Directions:

The teachers ask students to produce sounds with nonmusical objects in the classroom (chairs, pencils, shades, door, books, etc.). As the sound of each object is demonstrated, its name is written on the chalkboard. The objects are played on in the order in which they were mentioned. Vary the length of time for each object or play two together and create a chance composition.

Sound Categories

Ages: 6-8
Equipment: None
Directions:

After students have made a list of many things that make sounds, the teacher directs them to place the sounds in categories with similar characteristics. (Sounds that have a definite pitch, scraping sounds, clanging sounds, etc.)

Sounds 'N' Squares

Ages: 6-8
Equipment: Poster-sized paper
Directions:

The teacher draws a series of squares on the poster paper. It is the task of the students to suggest several different sound symbols to be placed in each square. When the chart is completed the composition can be performed by the class.

Variation: Each student can be assigned to make a single sound during the performance!

Tape the Tap

Ages: 6-8
Equipment: Tape recorder
Directions:

The teacher and students tape a variety of sounds around the school (water fountain, walking on stairs, ball bouncing on playground, chalk on board, etc.). The tape becomes a composition for the class. For a challenge students can create ways to write the music down to perform again.

Similar Sound

Ages: 6-8
Equipment: Rhythm instruments
Directions:

After students have become thoroughly familiar with the sound of each rhythm instrument, place several instruments on display. Similar, but different, instruments are given to the students. One student is chosen to be "it." "It" plays his instrument and then goes to the table and chooses an instrument that will sound most nearly like his own (rhythm sticks, claves, woodblocks or triangles, jingle clogs, finger cymbals, etc.).

Three-Level Sound

Ages: 6-8
Equipment: Prepared chalkboard
Directions:

The teacher prepares the chalkboard with a performance chart similar to the following one. The top line is performed in a high voice; the middle line in a medium voice; and the third line in a low voice. Sounds are made as indicated. Try recording this for a lot of fun!

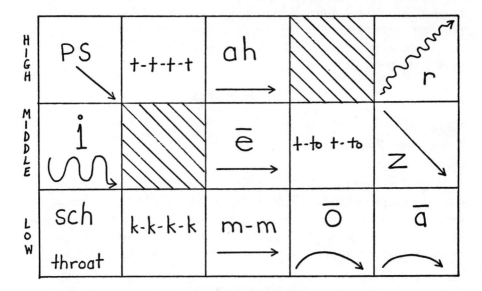

Sound Groups

Ages: 4-8
Equipment: Colored paper
Directions:

Students are divided into three groups, each assigned to a different task. One group may produce body sounds (head, upper torso, extremities); another may play rhythm instruments; the third may perform body movements. A color is assigned to each group. The teacher arranges papers of corresponding colors into a sequence for performance. The color arrangement sequence is displayed for all to see and the teacher leads a colorful performance of sound groups.

Name That Sound

Ages: 4-8
Equipment: A variety of sound-producing objects
Directions:

The challenge is to correctly name the sound in one hearing. A correct identification gives the student the reward of choosing the next player.

Match My Cylinder

Ages: 4-8
Equipment: Five pairs of sound cylinders
Directions:

The player spreads out all the sound cylinders and then listens to each one individually as he finds the matching pair. Vary the number of sound cylinders used in this game with the ability of the child.

Find Me

Ages: 4-8
Equipment: Rhythm instruments
Directions:

One player sits in front of the room with his back to the class. The other students are each given a rhythm instrument. The teacher chooses one student to play his instrument. It is the task of "it" to find the student who played.

Which Sound Is Different?

Ages: 4-8
Equipment: Three instruments that produce
different sounds
Directions:

Three sounds are played. In playing them the teacher should name "Sound Number One," "Sound Number Two," and "Sound Number Three." Two should be alike and one should be different. The student chosen to be "it" listens with covered face and then chooses which sound is different. A correct response might earn a paper badge which says "Good Listener."

Can You Change My Sound?

Ages: 4-8
Equipment: Sound-producing objects
Directions:

A student selects a sound-producing object and makes a sound. Another student is then chosen to use the same object but make a different sound. As many students may be chosen as ideas can be generated.

Circle the Sound

Ages: 4-8
Equipment: Pictures drawn on chalkboard
(as illustrated)
Directions:

The prepared pictures are on the chalkboard. The students are asked to point to different types of sound as requested. "Point to the low thumping sound," "Point to the instrument that makes a melody," "Point to the instrument that makes a high ringing sound," etc.

Variation: Work sheets may be prepared for each student.

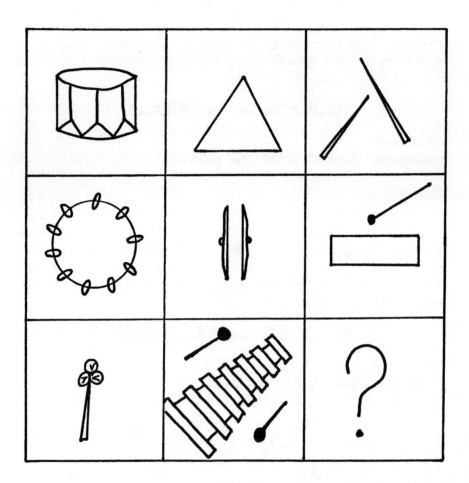

Sound stories play an important part in the listening and ear-training development of young children. Resources for these stories are abundant in books of children's stories.

Use:

Tongue twisters
Rhymes
Action songs
Picture-language books (rebuses)

Mystic Night

Grace Rowe
(a choral reading)

Group A: This is the night when the black cats prowl;
Group B: This is the night when the black cats yowl:
All: Me-ow! Me-ow-ow! Pst! pst!

Group A: This is the night when the brownies prance;
Group B: This is the night when the brownies dance;
All: Tip-tippy-tip! Tip-tippy-toe!

Group A: This is the night when the goblins moan;
Group B: This is the night when the goblins groan;
All: Yow-oo! Yow-oo! Yow-oo-oo-oo!

Group A: This is the night when the witches brew;
Group B: This is the night when the witches stew:
All: Mumble-dee-dee! Mumble-dee-do!

Group A: This is the night when the winds blow ill;
Group B: This is the night when the winds blow shrill:
All: Whoo-oo! Whoo-oo! Who-oo-oo!

Group A: This is the night when the lanterns leer;
Group B: This is the night when the lanterns jeer:
All: He-he-he! Ha-ha-ha! Ho-ho!

Group A: This is the mystic night of the year;
Group B: This is the mystic night we all fear:
All: Pst!! Me-ow!! Who-oo-oo!!

The Walk Home From School

(a sound story)

Directions: Students are directed to make an appropriate sound effect after each sentence.

As Marty neared home he was drawing farther and farther from the noise of the highway.

The noise of the trucks was fading away.

The squeal of the brakes was fading away.

Soon the only thing he heard was the twitter of birds.

As Marty walked slowly toward his home, the footpath seemed to crackle pleasantly with each step.

Marty could hear his heart beating with the joy of being alone on the country road.

He heard the rhythm of his horse, Smokey, running in the meadow.

He heard the bouncing of a rubber ball and he knew his little brother was near.

He knew that his mom would be in the kitchen making familiar cooking noises.

And Marty felt so happy and contented that it seemed his heart would burst with joy!

The Brave Young Indian

(a sound story)

Directions: Students are directed to make an appropriate sound effect after each sentence.

Many moons ago, in the land of the Plains Indian there was trouble.

The Chief called a conference of all the men of the village.

They gathered around the fire and discussed the problem until the fire dwindled to ashes.

Finally a young man stood up and volunteered to ride far off to find deer meat for the village.

Early the next morning the young man mounted his pony and rode off into the North Wind.

The young man and the pony rode on and on getting weaker and weaker.

Finally, they came upon a small water hole where there were two deer drinking.

The young man aimed his bow and arrow and let fly two direct hits.

When the young man returned home with the deer, there was great rejoicing in the village.

MAKING INSTRUMENTS

Many instruments can be made by students with very little assistance from the teacher. This manipulative experience helps the child explore the materials and the process of making sound. There is also a great deal of pleasure in creating something and being able to perform on your own instrument.

Young students can be quite successful at constructing string instruments (rubber-band harps and shoe-box guitars), wind instruments (soda-straw flutes and jug tubas), and percussion instruments (butter-tub shakers, coffee-can drums, sandpaper blocks, pie-tin cymbals, and scrap-lumber woodblocks). Of course the real fun of a homemade band is in the playing. Organize your band into sections: strings, winds and percussion. Have them play in groups. Be prepared for lots of learning from each other and for lots of fun with this activity. It may be good enough to share with parents!

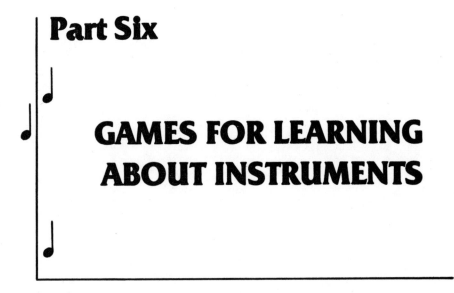

Part Six

GAMES FOR LEARNING ABOUT INSTRUMENTS

Learning About Instruments 167
Developing an Ensemble for Rhythm Instruments 178

LEARNING ABOUT INSTRUMENTS

For the young musician, learning about instruments involves two different tasks. One task is to explore and personally learn to perform on a variety of nonpitched and pitched rhythm instruments, both in accompanying and in a rhythm ensemble. The second task is to learn about instruments that would be played in a band or orchestra.

First, the *rhythm instruments*. After a child becomes familiar with exploring and experimenting with the sound producers, he or she is ready to play the classroom rhythm instruments.

The first time each instrument is introduced to the students should be a very special experience. Only one instrument should be introduced at a time and then carefully explored and enjoyed by each student. This should not be a rushed or hurried process but a very careful thought-provoking time so that the child may become thoroughly familiar with the instrument.

The first instruments generally introduced are the nontuned percussion instruments. Each one is introduced according to similarity of sound.

Recommended order for introducing instruments:

1. Tub drum or hand drum
2. Rhythm sticks
3. "Scraping" percussion (sandblocks)
4. "Striking" percussion (woodblocks, toneblocks)
5. "Shaking" percussion (tambourines, bells of indefinite pitch, maracas)
6. "Ringing" percussion (triangles, hand cymbals)
7. Then add melody instruments (step bells, diatonic bells, resonator bells and autoharp)

When instruments are added in this step-by-step method of exploration the child will become thoroughly familiar with the sight and sound of each one.

After each instrument has been introduced, the instruments may be used to accompany a familiar song. Young children love to accompany their favorite songs with their favorite instruments. Begin by using a simple ostinato or repetitive phrase. Remember to encourage students to create their own accompaniments, too. Use the instruments for small ensembles of similar sounds and then all together to form an instrumental ensemble.

Special rules may be developed by the students on handling the instruments. Children usually respect and feel very privileged to play an instrument.

Tips for using instruments in the classroom:

* Know what you expect the student to do with the instrument before you give it to him.
* Give clear, concise directions for performance.
* Label the shelves or drawers which house the instruments.
* Have student helpers care for the instruments.
* Use a system to let everyone have a turn.

Now for the *band and orchestra instruments*. These instruments are easily identified by sight and with careful listening they can be identified by their characteristic sound. The children can enjoy identifying and listening to them. As students become familiar with these instruments, they quickly develop their favorites. They can learn many things about the instruments.

* What do they sound like?
* What do they look like?
* How is the sound made?
* How is the instrument played?
* What size is the instrument?
* Is the pitch high or low?
* Do the students know someone who plays the instrument?
* Have the students seen the instrument at a concert?
* Did the students hear the instrument in the recording?
* Which instrument is their favorite? Why?

By the time a child reaches school age, he enjoys learning all about the band and orchestra instruments. Begin by introducing two instruments from each family of instruments to develop a familiarity of family timbre.

Percussion Family	Bass Drum and Snare Drum
String Family	Violin and Cello
Woodwind Family	Flute and Clarinet
Brass Family	Trumpet and Tuba

You will be amazed at how quickly students can identify the instrument by sight (both in actuality and by picture) and, with additional training, they can identify the instrument by timbre.

As the child progresses, he can add:

Percussion Family	Timpani
String Family	String Bass
Woodwind Family	Oboe and Bassoon
Brass Family	French Horn and Trombone

If an instrument is available, let the student experiment with holding it and learning how the sound is made. Sometimes an older brother or sister, or even parents, enjoy performing for classes. Encourage students to listen to concerts at school or in their community and develop a collection of good instrumental recordings to play often in your classroom.

Instrument Echo

Ages: 4-6
Equipment: Rhythm instruments
Directions:

The teacher chooses a player to be "it." "It" echoes the teacher's instrument pattern as this chant is called:

You see me!
I see you!

You hear me!
I hear you!

Play after me,
Do as I do.

(Student plays here)

Next person up
Will be you. (Choose a new "it")

What Shape Am I?

Ages: 4-6
Equipment: Colored paper in shapes of circles and triangles; cymbals, triangles and various drums (pictures or real instruments)
Directions:

One student is chosen to be "it." He moves his fingers around the edge of the shape chosen. It is his task to find an instrument that has the same shape. All types of drums are good to use as well as cymbals or triangles.

Set Them Up

Ages: 4-6
Equipment: Resonator bells
Directions:

Nine players are chosen for this game. Resonator bells are given to eight players (one bell on each tone of a scale) and the ninth player is "it." His task is to arrange the players so that the bells sound from low to high. When "it" is satisfied with the sound, he must ask the class if he is correct.

The Shapely Circus Band

Ages: 4-6
Equipment: Rhythm instruments
Colored paper in shapes of circles, triangles, squares and rectangles.
Directions:

The students construct a band performer from the different shapes of colored paper. This may be done as a class project on the flannel board or by individual students.

A Rhythm Story of Three Bears

Ages: 4-6
Equipment: None
Directions:

Make the appropriate rhythm pattern at the end of each line.

This is the Pa - pa Bear (clap)

This is the Ma - ma Bear (paschen)

This is Ba - by Bear (2 fingers)

This is go - ing for a walk (feet)

This is the love - ly day. (snap)

Once there was a Papa Bear
And there was a Mama Bear
Who had a little Baby Bear
And they went for a walk
On a very lovely day.
"What a pretty day," said Papa Bear.
"What a pretty day," said Mama Bear.
"It's O.K.," said Baby Bear,
And they walked and they walked,
It was such a lovely day.
"I could go all week," said Papa Bear.
"I could go all week," said Mama Bear.
"I'm tired," said Baby Bear.
But they kept on walking;
It was such a lovely day.
"Time to go home," said Papa Bear.
"Time to go home," said Mama Bear.
"Wanna go home," said Baby Bear.
And they turned and walked back home again.
The end of the lovely day.

Instrument Pantomime

Ages: 4-8
Equipment: None
Directions:

One student is chosen to be "it." He pantomimes the playing of an instrument of his choice. It is the task of a classmate to guess what instrument he was playing. A correct response brings a new "it."
Variation: This may be played as a team game!

Silent Orchestra

Ages: 4-8
Equipment: Recordings of instruments
Directions:

The teacher walks around a circle and whispers the name of an orchestral instrument to each player. As the sound of an instrument is heard on the recording, the person(s) with that instrument begin to play in pantomime. If an entire orchestra plays on the recording, all students play.

Mystery Instrument

Ages: 4-8
Equipment: Rhythm instruments
Directions:

All players shut their eyes. Several instruments are displayed. The leader plays several sounds on an instrument as everyone listens. The players then open their eyes and guess which instrument was played. The player with the correct answer becomes the new "it."

Hear and Name

Ages: 6-8
Equipment: Rhythm instruments
Directions:

The instruments to be used are displayed in the front of the room. One student is chosen to be "it." "It" is blindfolded or hides his eyes. A second student moves to any spot of his choice and plays one of the instruments. "It's" task is to walk to the instrument he has heard.

Instrument Match

Ages: 6-8
Equipment: Instrument pictures
Directions:

Pictures of instruments are placed in the front of the room. One student is chosen to group a family of instruments together. Another student is chosen to name the family. This is a good team game with each correct grouping and/or family name given a point.

Orchestra Around

Ages: 6-8
Equipment: Tags printed with names of orchestral instruments (one tag per student; 2-4 identical tags for each instrument used)
Directions:

Each student is given a tag with the name of an orchestral instrument on it. All players sit in a circle, except one who is "it." As he calls an instrument name, all players with that card change places. "It" will try to obtain a place in the circle and a new "it" will call a name of an instrument.

Variation: "It" may call instrument families; all instruments in the family must change.

Instrument Clue

Ages: 6-8
Equipment: None
Directions:

One player is chosen as "it." It is his task to describe an instrument to his classmates. He is to give one clue at a time and see how completely he can describe it.

Marching Band

Ages: 6-8
Equipment: Recordings of instruments
Prepared chalkboard or individual work sheets
Directions:

As the band instruments are played, a player comes to the board and draws an "x" through the instrument he has heard. If an individual game, the players may write the name of the instruments in the squares.

Variation: A team game may be developed to present a challenge!

BRASS	WOODWIND	PERCUSSION
Trumpet	Flute	Snare Drum
Trombone	Clarinet	Cymbals
Tuba	Saxophone	Bass Drum

Pick the Instrument

Ages: 6-8
Equipment: Pictures of instruments
                     Recordings of instruments
Directions:

The pictures of instruments are displayed at the front of the room. A recording of an instrument is played. A student is chosen to correctly identify the picture that belongs to the sound.

Name That Instrument

Ages: 6-8
Equipment: Rhythm instruments or pictures of instruments
Directions:

As the teacher displays an instrument, a student is chosen to name it correctly. This is a good game with which to choose instrument performers.

Circle Sounds

Ages: 6-8
Equipment: Cards showing different types of sounds
                     (whistling, birds, airplanes, etc.)
Directions:

The cards are given to selected players. One player is chosen to be the conductor. When the conductor points to the player, it is his task to make the sound on his card. What fun to tape this and create a sound composition!

What Did You Hear?

Ages: 6-8
Equipment: A variety of instruments
Directions:

Three instruments are chosen for the game. The teacher names the playing order. "It" is to play the three instruments in the order named. "It" is rewarded for a correct performance by choosing the next "it." This is excellent for reinforcing names of instruments.

Family Pair

Ages: 6-8
Equipment: Pictures of instruments
Directions:

Pictures of instruments are on display in the front of the room. The teacher calls the name of one instrument and the player chosen as "it" repeats the name of that instrument and must find another instrument picture from the same family.

Family Hang-Up

Ages: 6-8
Equipment: Pictures of instruments
Directions:

The chalkboard is prepared with areas designated for the four instrument families (strings, woodwind, brass and percussion). A stack of instrument pictures is placed at the front of the room. Each player in turn must pick up a picture and place it by the correct family name.

Variation: This may be played as a team game.

Music Treasure Hunt

Ages: 6-8
Equipment: Prepared notes*
         Treasure (we used candy in this example!)
Directions:

Hide the trail of notes and the treasure. Have fun!
*Instructions:

1. We're off on another Music Game—the last one for today.
   If you know musical instruments, it will be easy play.
   There is a certain instrument, (not very far from here)
   That conceals your next instructions, find maracas and
   you are near.
2. It's long and black and shiny; you play it with a reed.
   If you expect to end this game, its message you will need.
3. Its quality is fine; its family is String.
   If you look very closely, you'll find the next thing.
4. The highest of Brasses, quite close to the West;
   Have fun and enjoy it—this part may be best.
5. It's famous for its slide though it hangs along the wall.
   I think this music riddle may be the best of all.
6. Near a Tambourine and Bongo (believe it if you wish)
   You'll see a message in a drum that's acting like a dish.
7. Thanks so much for coming; we think you're pretty neat.
   Here's something to always remember: Hard work may end
   up sweet!

The Walking Casket

The Tale

Once upon a time, there was a walking casket. It was at least a trillion years old. The casket walked by day. And the casket walked by night. Whenever it came upon an unsuspecting victim, the door sprang open and out popped a Frankenstein-like monster. The monster was horrible. So horrible, the monster spread goose bumps up and down and all over his victims. And you know how that feels. This monster was a towering creature . . . at least 100 feet tall. And he always carried a flickering candle. The monster would wail and shriek eerily, paralyzing his victim with fright. Everyone was horrified. The monster actually turned his victims into mummies. Little sister and brother mummies. Big papa and mommy mummies. This terror went on for years and years. Would it ever stop? It seemed doubtful. Then one night a strange thing happened. The casket was making its regular rounds through the cemetery (the casket always paid a special visit to the cemetery at the stroke of midnight) when it came upon still another victim. A leprechaun, of all things. Well, thought the monster peering from his casket, here's a leprechaun I can take care of in short order. Out popped the monster from deep down within his casket. He carried on something fierce. Was the little leprechaun frightened? You bet your boots he was. But the determined little leprechaun wasn't about to be scared off by this ghostly monster. Not on your life. The leprechaun was going to outsmart the monster. The leprechaun raised himself up to his full two-foot, seven-inch height—the leprechaun was a real shorty—and with one mighty blow... what did he do? Did the leprechaun strike the monster square in the stomach? No. Did the leprechaun kick the monster in the shins? No. Did the leprechaun clobber the monster over the head? Nope. The brave little leprechaun—with one mighty blow—blew out the monster's candle. That did it. Without his candle, the monster had had it. The monster vanished in a puff of smoke. From that midnight on, no one ever saw the walking casket again. Everyone was happy.

Sound Effects

Directions:

    Make the suggested sound effect at each appropriate word.

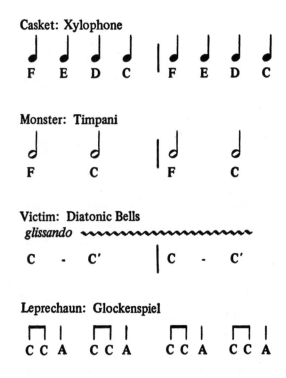

Casket: Xylophone

F E D C | F E D C

Monster: Timpani

F C | F C

Victim: Diatonic Bells
glissando ～～～～～～～～～～～～～～

C - C' | C - C'

Leprechaun: Glockenspiel

C C A   C C A   C C A   C C A

Candle: Sticks

Mummies: Metallophone

F   C   F   C

Midnight: Gong

(12 times)

DEVELOPING AN ENSEMBLE FOR RHYTHM INSTRUMENTS

Instruments should be introduced one at a time, giving each student familiarity with the sound and performance style before adding a new instrument. A logical and systematic presentation is:

1. Using the tub drum or hand drum.
2. Using rhythm sticks as an accompaniment to a song or in an ensemble.
3. Using scraping percussion instruments (sand blocks) as an accompaniment to a song or in an ensemble.
4. Playing striking percussion instruments (wood blocks or tone blocks) as an accompaniment or in an ensemble.
5. Playing shaking percussion instruments (headless tambourines, bells of indefinite pitch, maracas) as an accompaniment or in an ensemble.
6. Playing ringing percussion instruments (triangles, hand cymbals) in an accompaniment to a song or in an ensemble.
7. Playing the tambourine.
8. Playing the autoharp.
9. Playing diatonic bells.
10. Playing glockenspiels, xylophones, and metallophones.

Seating Arrangement for Instruments

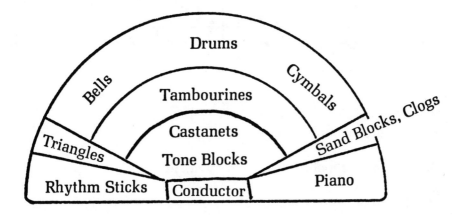

Writing a Score for Rhythm Ensembles

There are numerous ways to write a score for performing rhythm ensembles. Some well-used methods are:

Example 1:

	1	2	3	4	5	6	7	8
X	X	X	X	X	X	X	X	X
O	O			O				
△		△	△		△	△	△	△
✳	✳	✳		✳	✳		✳	✳

Example 2: (By color)

Red	Drums	
Green	Triangles	
Blue	Sticks	

Example 3: (Using the instrument shape as the symbol.)

	♩ ξ ξ	♩ ξ ξ ξ	♩ ξ ξ ξ	♩ ξ ξ ξ	♩ ξ ξ ξ	ξ ξ ξ
	♩	♩̄ ♩ ♩ ♩	♩̄ ♩ ♩ ♩	♩̄ ♩ ♩ ♩	♩̄ ♩ ♩ ♩	♩ ♩ ♩
	(ω)	♩ ω ω ω	♩ ω ω ω	♩ ω ω ω	♩ ω ω ω	ω ω ω

△   Picture symbol for the triangle.

   Picture symbol for the drum.

   Picture symbol for the finger cymbals.

   Picture symbol for the bells.

✕   Picture symbol for the sticks.

   Picture symbol for the tambourine.

⚡   Picture symbol for the maracas.

◠ ◠   Picture symbol for the coconut halves.

♗   Picture symbol for the castanets.

⬚⬚   Picture symbol for the African drums.

-◓ ◒-   Picture symbol for the cymbals.

🎵   Picture symbol for the guiro.

Example 4: (Following a line or circle for a graphic approach.)

Activities for an Ensemble of Rhythm Instruments

1. Students may echo the instrument and pattern from the teacher.
2. Students may play musical "conversations" in phrases to each other.
3. Students may play same and different phrases with the teacher or other students.
4. Use rhythm instruments to perform different musical forms: AB, ABA; Rondo; Theme and Variations; or Introduction/Coda.
5. Use instruments to perform an ostinato to a familiar song.
6. Create talent shows in the classroom to perform with the rhythm ensemble.
7. Students may play along with a recording of music literature. *Example:* "Hall of the Mountain King"
8. Use changes in tempo.
9. Use changes in the dynamic level by having the conductor open arms wide for loud and close arms for soft.
10. Use delicate staccato notes and accents to vary the sound.
11. Use a dial that has a hand pointing to loud and soft to change dynamic levels.
12. When the conductor's hands are high in the air, the high-pitched instruments play; when the conductor's hands are low to the floor, the low-pitched instruments play.
13. Students think their part silently before playing (audiate), or tap on knee.
14. Use a rest position before each composition.
15. Use groups of similar-sounding instruments.
16. Alternate phrases or sections between groups of instruments.

Part Seven

LEARNING CENTERS

Where and When 186
Using Them 186
Designing Them 187
Learning Centers for Listening to Music 188
Learning Centers for Sound Exploration 192
Learning Centers for Exploring Instruments 196
Learning Centers for Singing 200
Learning Centers for Music Writing 203
Learning Centers for Other Activities 207

In this section we will refer to learning centers as any means of organizing instruction so that students can direct much of their own learning. Any bulletin board, table, wall, or corner that is prepared with instructional stimulators and information for student activity is a learning center.

A major objective of learning centers is enabling the student to become a self-directed learner. Learning centers may be designed to require that students do any or all of the following: choose objectives, select materials, develop projects, share projects, and evaluate the experience. Each one of those tasks promotes independence in the learner and is excellent for encouraging initiative and integrity of the student.

Music for young children is traditionally scheduled into set portions of time and in a designated music room. In that situation, learning centers have limited use and limited opportunities. But we advocate the outpouring of music into the entire school so that a variety of music corners and music learning centers can be established in many nooks and corners throughout the school.

The element of sound as encountered in the development of music centers will be reckoned with along with suggested materials, procedures and complete directions for self-directed activities for young children.

Directions for a learning center should be minimal. Children can teach themselves many things as well as gain much information from each other. Let the children explore and discover, giving help only when necessary. Post instructions at each learning center. In addition, introduce and demonstrate the use of the center to each class. This introduction will acquaint them with the goals and objectives of the center and it will provide needed instructions to the ones who are too young or unskilled to read.

How much self-directed activity can a young student accomplish? Such a question can be answered only by the accomplishments of the child himself. Set no limits! Provide opportunities for the student and then you will know what he can accomplish on his own. Set up learning centers and let the learning happen!

LEARNING CENTERS: WHERE AND WHEN

Learning centers for musical experiences are useful throughout the school environment, sometimes offering opportunity for experimenting and exploring, sometimes offering opportunity for improving skills, sometimes offering opportunity for enrichment and learning. The presence of music corners throughout the school can help to promote a child's self-concept and his appreciation of others, as well as his appreciation of music.

Music learning centers should be strategically placed in the school so that they are accessible and, at the same time, offer some degree of privacy to the working student. Some classroom teachers will be very pleased to have the music teacher place a learning center in the classroom. In this case the classroom teacher will provide the space; the music teacher should take complete responsibility for providing and arranging materials in the center. The classroom teacher will assume responsibility for monitoring the center and for establishing guidelines as to when students may use it.

Some school librarians or media specialists will be delighted to have a music learning center in their library or media center. Here, again, the music teacher should assume full responsibility for assembling the center; the librarian or media specialist will supervise the use of it.

The music teacher will probably need to assume full responsibility for monitoring learning centers that may be located in multiuse activity rooms or hallways. Certainly the music teacher will be responsible for centers which are set up in the music room.

Different teachers may want to establish different rules as to when students may work at learning centers. Some will design them to be used before and after school, at recess and during free time. Others may designate only certain periods of the week for their availability. Still others will make them available at any time. Discover what is best for your needs and plan accordingly.

LEARNING CENTERS: USING THEM

Some music teachers have effectively established one music learning center in the school library, two in the music room, and additional centers in six classrooms. The six classrooms are often set up so that the learning centers rotate among them, enabling each classroom to have the center for a few weeks before moving it on to the next classroom. In this system of rotation the music teacher initially creates six centers and then simply assumes responsibility for maintaining them and rotating them every few weeks.

All of the music learning centers will need to be changed or freshened about once a month. A teacher with planning time can easily create two or three new centers each month, sometimes being completely original and sometimes using things from a previous year. On occasion the older students can be very helpful in designing and implementing learning centers. Student involvement, of course, always creates a greater feeling of pride and respect in the students, and is recommended when it is feasible.

Each learning center must be introduced and demonstrated first to the entire class. Take some class time to do this and be sure that all of the students understand the purposes and expectations of the center. After this initial presentation to the large group the center may be moved to its designated place ready to receive its eager experimentalists and learners.

The privilege of working at a learning center is sometimes given to students as a reward for good performance or good behavior; sometimes it is offered as an enrichment to those who finish their other work first. Some teachers are more comfortable in using a system that requires students to sign up for their turn at the learning center. Discover the plan that works best for your purposes and make the system your own. The purpose is not to be encumbered, but to be free for facilitating learning.

LEARNING CENTERS: DESIGNING THEM

Design each learning center so that it is pleasant, cheerful and complete with the materials needed for its particular experience. Some learning centers may need to contain desks and chairs; others may need floor space; some work well on the carpet with pillows tossed around; still others will need a worktable. Every learning center should be highlighted with posters or colorful pictures. Every learning center should also contain an instruction chart. Even students who cannot read will rely on someone explaining the content of the instruction chart.

Developing learning centers can be a very creative experience for teachers. In the name of learning centers all kinds of boxes have been brought into modern schools. Also used have been bathtubs, dishpans, rocking chairs, old shoes, and dressmaker's cardboard cutting boards. Be limited only by your imagination. Borrow ideas from other teachers. Adapt and adopt! Be inventive in designing your own learning centers!

LEARNING CENTERS FOR LISTENING TO MUSIC

Learning centers for listening to music are quiet centers. Each center will require headphones and a record or tape player. Each center may serve an individual or a small group. Because these are quiet centers they may be placed anywhere in the school, preferably apart from high-energy activities. Suggested locations are: the classroom, the music room, the media center, or any activity room.

Decorate the listening centers with attractive posters, pictures, and posted reminders to "Listen Quietly," "Hear the Instruments," and "Enjoy!"

A Music Center for "Let's Pretend"

Materials displayed

* A "Pretend Box" filled with hats, ribbons, scarves, cloths, etc.
* Two or three recordings of short, dramatic pieces of music.

Instructions posted

1. Select a piece of music from those provided.
2. Listen carefully to decide which costumes and actions would be best suited for it.
3. Take what you need from the Pretend Box.
4. Quietly act out your idea with the music.
5. When you have finished, put everything away.

A Story-Book Center for Music Listening

Materials displayed

* A library book that presents one of the well-known music classics such as Nutcracker Suite, William Tell, Froggie Went A Courtin', etc.
* A record to correlate with the book selected.

Instructions posted

1. Read the story book while you listen to the music.
2. Does it seem to you that the music and the story go well together?
3. Why or why not?

A Listening Center for Patriotic Music

Materials displayed

* Pictures of patriotic events and the national flag.
* Library books on patriotism.
* Three or four records of patriotic music such as, "The Star Spangled Banner," "America," "The Stars and Stripes Forever," and "You're A Grand Old Flag."

Instructions posted

1. Do you know music about your country? Listen to these.
2. Tell which piece is your favorite. Why?
3. Can you sing a song about your country?

A Listening Center for the Waltz

Materials displayed

* Pictures of swirling dancers.
* Some small dolls dressed in ballgowns.
* Two or three recordings of waltz music.

Instructions posted

1. Listen to music of the waltz.
2. Make the dolls sway in rhythm to the music.
3. Can you dance the waltz?

A Listening Center for Marches

Materials displayed

* Pictures of marching bands.
* Two or three recordings of marches.

Instructions posted:

1. Listen to march music.
2. Keep the beat quietly in your hand or in your toe.
3. Can you imagine a parade marching by? Or a football show?

A Listening Center with Art

Materials displayed

* Drawing paper, crayons, colored paper, scissors.
* Two or three recordings of music that offer contrasts in mood and spirit.

Instructions posted

1. Listen to one of the records provided.
2. Illustrate what it represents or how it makes you feel.
3. Share your artwork with a friend. Post it at this center.

A Listening Center with a Filmstrip

Materials displayed

* Filmstrip viewer and filmstrip.
* Correlated record (check your audiovisual catalogues for filmstrip-record sets of music literature).

Instructions posted

1. View a filmstrip with a record.
2. Did it suit your fancy?

A Listening Center with Puppets

Materials displayed

* Two or three hand puppets with movable mouths.
* Two or three recordings of short, dramatic, instrumental selections or songs.

Instructions posted

1. Listen to one of the records provided.
2. Have the puppets act a story to match the music (or have the puppets sing with the record).
3. Present your puppet show to the entire class!

A Listening Center

Materials displayed

* A selection of records that contain both familiar and unfamiliar pieces.

Instructions posted

1. Choose any record you like.
2. Listen quietly and enjoy it.

A Listening Center for Latin American Music

Materials displayed

* Pictures of Latin American dancers and instruments.
* Maracas
* A recording of lively Latin American music.

Instructions posted

1. Listen to the Latin American music.
2. Play along with the maracas.
3. Imagine the fun of the dancers!

A Listening Center for Oriental Music

Materials displayed

* Pictures representative of Oriental cultures.
* A recording of an Oriental song.

Instructions posted

1. Listen to the Oriental music.
2. Can you move your hands as the Oriental dancers do?
3. Can you sing the Oriental song?

A Listening Center to Hear Bands, Orchestras and Choirs

Materials displayed

* A cassette player.
* Three prepared cassettes: one each for band, orchestra and choir.
* Pictures of bands, orchestras and choirs.

Instructions posted

1. Can you identify the sound of a band? orchestra? choir?
2. Listen to each tape to see if you can tell which is which. The correct answer will be given at the end of each tape.
3. Listen to each tape again just for fun!

LEARNING CENTERS FOR SOUND EXPLORATION

Learning centers for sound exploration will be centers that create sound. Some of them will involve two students at a time. Consider placing these centers in a spot that does not require total silence but that does offer some privacy. The privacy may be achieved by utilizing a study carrell, three sides of a large cardboard box, or an area set apart by a screen. Suggested locations are: a corner of the music room, a corner of the classroom, a corner of the media center, a corner of the cafeteria, or a corner of any activity room.

Make the learning center attractive by decorating with colorful paper, posters and pictures.

A Learning Center for Sound Boxes

Materials displayed

* A dozen or so match boxes (or other boxes near that size) that have each had a small amount of sound material placed inside. Suggested sound materials are rice, paper clips, beans, and macaroni.

Instructions posted

1. Which box makes the softest sound?
2. Which box makes the loudest sound?
3. Arrange the boxes in order from softest to loudest.
4. Ask a friend to check.

✓ A Learning Center Sound-Guessing Game

Materials displayed

* An empty soup can.
* A tray containing several sound-producing objects such as a large screw, a button, a plastic chip, a rubber eraser, and a penny.

Instructions posted

1. Place one object into the can. Listen to its sound as you shake it.
2. Listen to each sound as you place the objects, one by one, into the can.

3. Turn your back while a friend chooses an object and shakes it in the can for you. Listen carefully.
4. Can you guess which object your friend chose?
5. After you have three turns, trade places with your friend.
6. Are you very good at this game? How about your friend?

Autumn Center

Materials displayed
* Pictures of autumn scenes.
* Walnut shells.

Instructions posted
1. How many different sounds can you make from the walnut shells?
2. Make a song about the picture or the shells.
3. Play and sing your song for someone.

Sound-Matching Center

Materials displayed
* Several matching pairs of sound cylinders.

Instructions posted
1. Listen carefully to each sound cylinder.
2. Can you find the matching pairs?
3. Check your work.

Sound-Categorizing Center

Materials displayed
* A random arrangement of four or five pairs of similar-sounding instruments such as wood block and tone block, rhythm sticks and claves, two kinds of drums, maracas and headless tambourine, triangle and finger cymbals.

Instructions posted
1. Listen carefully to the sounds of each instrument.
2. Find two instruments that sound similar. Why are they nearly the same?

3. Find two other instruments that sound similar. Why are they alike?
4. Continue until each instrument has a similar-sounding partner.
5. Can you tell why some are alike and some are different?

A Discovering Sound Center

Materials displayed

* A small drumstick and a piece of heavy cardboard (an old gameboard is ideal) which has been prepared with various pieces of sound-producing material such as sandpaper, a small scrap of lumber, a square of corrugated cardboard, a metal jar lid, a small metal can, or a plastic lid.

Instructions posted

1. How many different sounds can you find here?
2. Make your own composition and share it with a friend.

A Maracas Sound Center

Materials displayed

* One maraca and photographs or drawings representing gentle rainfall, hard rainfall and Latin American dancers.

Instructions posted

1. Can you make a maraca sound for each picture?
2. Share your ideas with a friend.

A Sound-Amplification Center

Materials displayed

* A large cardboard tube, a small cardboard tube, a maraca, and one small jingle bell.

Instructions posted

1. Hold the small tube to your ear and play the maraca into the tube. How does it sound?
2. Hold the large tube to your ear and play the maraca into the tube. How does that sound?

3. Compare the sound of the two tubes. What makes them different?
4. Repeat the experiment with the jingle bell and each tube.
5. Compare your opinions with those of a friend.

A Rubber Band Center

Materials displayed

* A small board with small nails spaced at different intervals and a variety of rubber bands.

Instructions posted

1. Stretch a rubber band between two nails; pluck it and listen to the sound.
2. Stretch rubber bands of various sizes into various lengths.
3. Compare the sounds of the different ones.
4. Can you make a musical composition with the rubber bands?

A Drum Center

Materials displayed

* A small drumstick with a variety of homemade drums such as oatmeal boxes, plastic tubs, coffee cans and shoe boxes.

Instructions posted

1. Play each drum softly.
2. Compare the sounds.
3. Which sound do you prefer Why?
4. Can you make a piece of music for the drums?

A Sound-Experiment Center

Materials displayed

* Two or three small plastic butter tubs.
* Several containers each with different sound materials such as sand, rice, noodles, plastic chips, metal screws, cardboard pieces, etc.

Instructions posted

1. Put some rice into a plastic tub; seal securely. Shake it and listen to its sound.
2. Pour some screws into another plastic tub; seal it securely. Shake it and listen to its sound.
3. Do you prefer the sound of the rice or the screws?
4. Empty the plastic tubs and experiment with some other sounds.
5. Name your favorite sound materials and tell why.

A Listening Center

Materials displayed

* One resonator bell (any note from the C Major scale, except C).
* One set of diatonic bells.

Instructions posted

1. Play the resonator bell.
2. Find the sound that matches it from the other bells.
3. Ask a friend to check.

Bell Center

Materials displayed

* One set of diatonic bells with soft mallet.

Instructions posted

1. Play a pattern moving UP.
2. Play a pattern moving DOWN.
3. Play a pattern moving SAME.
4. Ask a friend to check.

LEARNING CENTERS FOR EXPLORING INSTRUMENTS

Learning centers for playing instruments will be centers that create sound. Consider placing them in a spot that does not require total silence but that does offer some privacy. The privacy may be achieved by utilizing a study carrell, three sides of a large cardboard box, or an area set apart by a screen. Suggested locations are: a corner of the music room, a corner of the classroom, a corner of the media center, or a corner of any activity room.

Instrument centers may be attractively decorated with appropriate pictures as well as card captions reminding students to "Play Softly," "Listen Carefully," "Play Correctly," and "Have Fun!"

An Autoharp Center

Materials displayed
* Autoharp and pick.

Instructions posted
1. Play G Chord four times.
2. Play D^7 Chord four times.
3. Play G Chord four times again.
4. Ask a friend to check.
5. Make up your own song!

An Orchestra Center

Materials displayed
* Pictures of orchestral instruments.

Instructions posted
1. Put the pictures of string instruments together.
2. Put the pictures of brass instruments together.
3. Put the pictures of percussion instruments together.
4. Put the pictures of woodwind instruments together.
5. Ask a friend to check.

A Resonator-Bell Center

Materials displayed
* Several resonator bells (your choice).
* A mallet.

Instructions posted
1. Can you find a familiar song on the Resonator Bells?
2. Can you find a new song on the Resonator Bells?
3. Have fun!

A Piano Center

Materials displayed

> * A cardboard keyboard, an electric keyboard, or a real piano.

Instructions posted

> 1. Play all of the black keys.
> 2. Play all of the white keys.
> 3. Make up a song on a few black keys.
> 4. Make up a song on a few white keys.
> 5. Have fun!

A Violin Center

Materials displayed

> * A small violin and bow.
> * A picture of correct violin posture.

Instructions posted

> 1. Hold the violin as in the picture.
> 2. Play a few notes on each string with the bow.
> 3. Pluck a few notes on each string (pizzicato).
> 4. Can you make a tune on the violin?

A Ukulele Center

Materials displayed

> * A ukulele.
> * A picture of correct ukulele posture.
> * Picture cards showing two or three basic chord positions.

Instructions posted

> 1. Hold the ukulele as in the picture.
> 2. Learn to play one of the chords pictured.
> 3. Learn to play the other chords given.
> 4. Play a song you know like "Aunt Rhody," "Billy Boy," or "Old Joe Clark." Sing while you play.

A Center for Playing Any Instrument

Materials displayed

* Any available instrument (such as tambourine, temple blocks, glockenspiel, finger cymbals, tick-tock blocks, etc.).
* Pictures relevant to the instrument (optional).

Instructions posted

1. Do you know the name of this instrument?
2. Can you play it?
3. Can you make a song on it?

A Center for Playing Diatonic Bells

Materials displayed

* A set of diatonic bells and mallet.

Instructions posted

1. Play all of the bars.
2. Count how many bars are on this set of bells.
3. Play and count the bars as you play. Start at the lowest sound and go up the scale to the highest sound.
4. Play the bars starting at the highest sound and go down the scale to the lowest sound.
5. Create your own tune.

An Art Center

Materials displayed

* Magazines containing music pictures.
* Poster board, scissors, paste.

Instructions posted

1. Look at one of the magazines and cut out pictures of musical instruments.
2. Glue them on the board in any order.
3. Share your collage with the class.

LEARNING CENTERS FOR SINGING

Learning centers for singing will be centers that create sound. Some of them will involve two students at the same time. Consider placing them in a spot that does not require total silence but that does offer some privacy. The privacy may be achieved by utilizing a study carrell, three sides of a large cardboard box, or an area set apart by a screen. Suggested locations are: a corner of the music room, a corner of the classroom, a corner of the media center, or a corner of any activity room.

The centers for singing may be decorated with attractive pictures and posters of people singing. Make it a bright and cheerful spot!

A Center for Harry the Hose

Materials displayed

* A soft hose as from a vacuum cleaner or hair dryer (this may be decorated with glued-on ear and face features).

Instructions posted

1. Listen to Harry the Hose as he sings to you.
2. Place Harry's ear near your mouth; sing softly to him.
3. Place Harry's mouth near your ear; can you hear the singing?
4. Softly sing your favorite song for Harry. Is it in tune?
5. Have fun with Harry the Hose!

A Center for Singing Puppets

Materials displayed

* Two or three hand puppets (any characters will do).

Instructions posted

1. Let the puppets sing with your voice.
2. Can you open and close their mouth at all the right times to fit the song?
3. The puppets would like to sing all of your favorite songs!
4. Sometimes two puppets like to take turns singing alternate lines of the same song.
5. These puppets especially like to sing songs about animals.

A Center for Singing a Story

Materials displayed

    * Some colorful easy-reading story books, especially ones with conversation.

Instructions posted

1. Select the book of your choice to sing.
2. Sing the whole story to yourself.
3. Can you make different voice sounds for the different parts of the story?
4. Would you like to sing your story to a friend?

A Center for Making a Song

Materials displayed

    * A cassette tape recorder.
    * Some seasonal stimulators (one season at a time) such as colored leaves for fall, budding plants for spring, holiday items for winter, vacation pictures for summer.

Instructions posted

1. Make a song about the season. Sing it again.
2. Sing your song into the tape recorder.
3. Share the tape with a friend.
4. Can your teacher help you write your song?

A Center for a Record Sing-a-Long

Materials displayed

    * Two or three recordings of favorite songs.
    * A record player (headphones, optional)

Instructions posted

1. Select a record from those provided.
2. Sing along with your record.
3. Do you know all the words to the song?
4. How many songs can you sing along?

A Center for Singing a Scale Song

Materials displayed

* A set of diatonic bells with mallet.
* Words for a familiar scale tone song.

Instructions posted

1. Play your diatonic bells beginning at the lowest note and play each bar until you get to the highest note.
2. Choose the song you want to sing.
3. Sing and play your favorite scale tone song.

Examples of scale tone songs to use

Autumn Leaves

Down,
Down
Yellow and
Brown
Leaves are
Falling
On the
Ground

Rake them
Up in a
Pile so
High
Till they
Nearly
Reach the
Sky

Jump in the
Middle and
Roll all a-
round
Play in the
Leaves and then
Toss them a-
round

Back to your
Place now, You're
not a bit hurt
Stand right here
Now and we'll
Brush off the
Dirt

Halloween

There was a ghost on Halloween
He lived behind the house
He spooked around the corners just as
Quiet as a mouse
He floated through the walls and through the
Doors and windows, too
And everytime he saw someone
He made a great big "Boo!"
Boo, Booo, Booo, Booo, Booo,
    Booo, Booo, Boo!

A Center for a Singing Game

Materials displayed

* One blindfold or large handkerchief.
* Five small objects such as pencil, crayon, eraser, chalk, pen (place them on a small tray).

Instructions posted

1. Find a friend to play this singing game.
2. Study the objects on the tray.
3. Put on the blindfold or cover your eyes.
4. Ask your friend to choose one object; then you guess which one it is by singing, "Do you have the pencil?" or "Do you have the eraser?" or another object.
5. When you have guessed correctly, trade places with your friend.

LEARNING CENTERS FOR MUSIC WRITING

Learning centers for music writing are quiet centers. Each center will require space that students may use as a writing area. Each center may serve an individual or a small group (two or three). Because these are quiet centers they may be placed anywhere in the school, preferably apart from high-energy activities. Suggested locations are: the classroom, the music room, the media center, or any activity room.

Decorate the music-writing centers with attractive posters, pictures, and posted reminders to "Write Carefully," "Think!" "Be a Composer," "Be A Music Maker," and "Have Fun With Music!"

A Notation Center

Materials displayed

* Flannel board with music staff.
* Four note heads.

Instructions posted

1. Place the notes LOW on the staff.
2. Place the notes HIGH on the staff.
3. Place the notes moving UP on the staff.
4. Place the notes moving DOWN on the staff.
5. Ask a friend to check.

A Center for Matching a Music Pattern

Materials displayed

* Flannel board with two music staffs; the upper staff should be prepared with six or eight notes in a melodic pattern.
* An equal number of additional notes should be available.

Instructions posted

1. Study the melody pattern given on the flannel board.
2. Arrange notes on the lower staff so that they match the first one.
3. Ask a friend to check your work.

A Center for Writing Scales

Materials displayed

* Work sheets for students (two or three incomplete scales and one blank staff).
* An example of a finished work sheet.
* Pencils.

Instructions posted

1. Complete the scales on the work sheet.
2. Write an entire scale on the staff provided.
3. Check your work. (How many notes are in a scale? Did you use every line and every space?)

A Center for Writing Rhythm Patterns

Materials displayed

* A cassette player with prepared tape of ten rhythm patterns studied.
* Headphones.
* Writing paper and pencil.

Instructions posted

1. Listen to the tape of rhythm patterns.
2. Write each pattern as you hear it.
3. Ask your teacher for the answer sheet so that you can check your work.
4. Listen again to find your mistakes.
5. Were you perfect?

A Center for Writing Directional Melody Patterns

Materials displayed

* A poster of arrows in every direction.
* Manuscript paper.
* Pencils.

Instructions posted

1. Write note patterns that move upward. (Put five or more notes in each pattern).
2. Write a note pattern that moves downward. (Five or more notes).
3. Write a note pattern that moves across. (Five or more notes).
4. Write a note pattern that moves up and down. (Ten or more notes).
5. Can you sing the patterns that you have written?
6. Do it again!

A Music-Writing Center with Musical Magic Slates

Materials displayed

* One or two musical magic slates (available from school supply catalogues).
* A primary song book.

Instructions posted

1. Practice writing music on the musical magic slate. Erase.
2. Choose a song to copy from the song book.
3. Copy your song onto the musical magic slate.
4. Ask a friend to check your work.
5. When you run out of space, clear the slate and continue.
6. Have fun with music magic!

A Center for Copying Music Symbols

Materials displayed

* A poster of basic music symbols: treble clef, eighth note, quarter note, half note, whole note, quarter rest, half rest, and whole rest.
* Writing paper and pencil.

Instructions posted

1. Copy each of the symbols posted.
2. Make several examples of each symbol.
3. Which symbol is the most fun to draw?
4. Fill up your paper practicing the music symbols. (Do the other side, too.)
5. Enjoy!

A Center for Writing a Composition

Materials displayed

* Music manuscript paper with four staffs.
* Pencils.

Instructions posted

1. Number your music staffs like this: 1, 2, 3, 4.
2. On Staff No. 1 write a note pattern that uses seven notes.
3. On Staff No. 2 write a note pattern that is exactly like No. 1.
4. On Staff No. 3 write a note pattern that is different from the others; it should use ten or eleven notes.
5. On Staff No. 4 repeat the note pattern that is exactly like No. 1.
6. Ask your teacher to help you play your piece on the bells. Talk about the organization of your piece.

A Center for Writing Note Words

Materials displayed

* Music manuscript paper and pencil.
* A poster that gives note names in treble (and bass) clefs.
* A list of words that may be spelled with the musical alphabet. (egg, bed, bad, fed, gag, beef, cage, bead, face, fade, etc.)
* Answer Sheet with same words written on music staff.

Instructions posted

1. Write the words given on the music staff.
2. Check your work with the answer sheet.
3. Were you perfect?

4. Make a secret code using words written on the music staff.
5. Be sophisticated!

LEARNING CENTERS FOR OTHER ACTIVITIES

A Learning Center for Matching Note Cards

Materials displayed

* A set of music note cards (treble clef, bass clef, or both).

Instructions posted

1. Look carefully at the music note cards to find the matching pairs.
2. How many matching pairs can you find?
3. How quickly can you find all of the matching pairs?
4. Be careful!

A Tactile Learning Center for Music

Materials displayed

* A set of tactile music cards

Instructions posted

1. Close your eyes to feel each music card.
2. Can you identify each music symbol?
3. Can you close your eyes and find matched pairs?
4. Do your fingers have eyes?

A Rhythm Center

Materials displayed

* Sticks for rhythmic stick notation (popsicle sticks or straws).

Instructions posted

1. Take the sticks and write this rhythm pattern. Clap it.
2. Take the sticks and write this rhythm pattern. Clap it.
3. Take the sticks and write this rhythm pattern. Clap it.
4. Write a rhythm pattern of your own. Clap it.

A Sol-Mi Center

Materials displayed

* A small box containing six pieces of string and circular foam packing pieces.

Instructions posted

1. Take five pieces of string and place them on the table to make a staff.
2. Take one piece of string and make a treble clef for your staff.
3. Place a foam piece note on second space "A".
4. Place a foam piece note on first space "F".
5. Can you find other sol-mi notes?

APPENDIX

How to Make Suggested Equipment

Arrow Cards

Materials: A set of 6 cards (3" x 5") for each direction marking pen

Directions: On each card, draw a directional arrow as follows:
Two cards with an ascending arrow
Two cards with a descending arrow
Two cards with a horizontal arrow.

Bean Bags

Materials: Durable cotton material
Beans

Directions: Cut two 12" circles for each bean bag.
Sew ½" seam tightly around the circle, leaving an opening for filling with the beans. Clip the seam. Turn inside out.
Insert the beans. Sew the opening securely.

Circle Cards

Materials: Construction paper circles
Magic markers

Directions: Cut six or eight circles (8" diameter) from the construction paper. On each circle of paper, draw a picture of an object that makes a noise (whistle, birds, airplanes, bee, etc.).

Floor Staff

Materials: Scotch tape #471, 2″ wide, any color

Directions: Using the tape, make a staff on the floor. Use as much length as your room allows. Place the lines so that there are about twelve inches of space between each line. You may want to add the treble clef to the staff with the same tape.

A Feely Box

Materials: A cardboard box (approximately 10″ x 15″)
Sound-producing items, such as two small sticks, two small rattles, two scraps of sandpaper, two dried pods, etc.

Directions: The cardboard box may be attractively decorated in any manner. Cut an opening in the box, in an appropriate size for a young hand to reach through. Place two each of the sound-producing items inside the box. For a special effect, use a fringe of paper or yarn strands over the opening.

Melody Cards

Materials: Twelve cards (approximately 8¼″ x 11″)
Marking pen

Directions: Draw a staff and a treble clef on each card. Write a different four or five note melody on each card. Be sure that you make three melodies ascending, three melodies descending, and three melodies with repeated tones.

Note Discs

Materials: Heavy construction paper

Directions: Cut 10″ circles from the heavy construction paper to form a note disc. Discs may be made of wood or cardboard and painted black for greater durability and realism.

Sound Cylinders

Materials: 32 sturdy paper cups or tin cans
Masking tape

Colored markers
Sound-producing materials, such as rice, sand, beans, pebbles, macaroni, peas, marbles, etc.

Directions: Into two of the cups put a small amount of rice; into two more cups put a small amount of sand; into two more cups put a small amount of beans, etc. Continue in this manner until half of the cups contain some sound material. Using the remaining cups to turn upside-down over the filled cups, fasten each cylinder securely by wrapping masking tape around the cups at the point where they meet. On the bottom of each sound cylinder place a small colored dot. Use a different colored dot for each pair of sound cylinders for student self-checking.

Set-a-Pattern Cards

Materials: A set of 12 cards (3″ x 5″)
Marking pen

Directions: On four of the cards write "skip"
On four of the cards, write "step"
On four of the cards write "repeat."

3-D Music Symbol Cards

Materials: 20 flash cards
Marking pen
Sandpaper or felt material
Scissors and glue

Directions: Draw and cut, from either the sandpaper or felt, two sets of each of the following symbols:

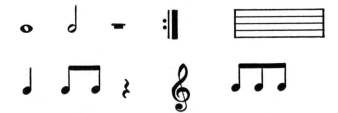

ALPHABETICAL INDEX

A

All Around the Kitchen, 66
Animal Sounds, 153
Airport, 25
Airport, Let's Pretend a Trip to, 25
Amusement Park, Let's Pretend a Trip to
    an, 26
Arrows on Bells, 86
Art Center, An, 199
Art, A Listening Center with, 191
Art, A Gallery of, 22
As Quiet As, 20
Autoharp Center, 197
Autumn Center, 193

B

Bean Dip, 34
Beat Parade, 36
Being a Melody, 82
Bell Center, 196
Bluebird, Bluebird, 70
Bounce and Hum, 105
Bouncing Ball, 17
Bow, Bow, Bow Belinda, 74
Breathe a Jive, 106
Bunny's Hop, 45

C

Can You Change My Sound?, 159
Can You Hear My Step?, 82
Career Clue, 115
Catch My Tempo, 35
Chance, By, 156
Change the Keys, 106
Change the Verse, 100
Choir, Classroom, 111
Circle Around, 89
Circle Sounds, 174
Circle the Sound, 160
Circus Band, The Shapely, 170
Circus Parade, The, 31
City, This Is the, 30
Clap Your Hands, 55
Climbing Note Mountain, 85
Composer Chant, 146

Composer Train, 146
Concert Time, 111
Conversation Opera, 114
Copy Cat, 22
Create a Verse, 115

D

Dancing Kids, 18
Diatonic Bells, A Center for Playing, 199
Did You Ever See a Lassie, 68
Directions, 21
Drama, A Music, 24
Drum Center, A, 195
Drum Echoes, 38

E

Echo Down the Line, 104
Echo My Pattern, 83
Environmental Chant, 34

F

Family Hang-Up, 175
Family Pair, 175
Farm, This Is the, 29
Farmer in the Dell, 57
Feel and Find Box, 86
Field Trip, Our, 30
Filmstrip, Learning Center with a, 190
Find Me, 159
Find My Sound, 153
Finger March, 33
Follow, Follow Me, 43
Follow the Leader, 19
Football Game, At the, 18
Freeway, The, 18
Funny Freeze, 41

G

Galloping Ponies in the Ring, 42
Gerbil Music, 155
Getting Into a Circle, 40
Getting on the Beam, 105
Guess Who?, 108

H

Halloween Night, 99
Halloween Night, 104
Hands and Arms—Not Legs or Mouth, 20
Hands Only, For, 19
Hands Up High, 82
Harry the Hose, A Center for, 200
Hear and Name, 172,
Hear and Write, 92
Hearing Hose, A, 103
Here We Go, Santy Malone, 54
Hey, Betty Martin, 65
Hide the Beat, 33
High/Low, 81
High and Low Sounds, 154
Hit Parade, 110
Hokey Pokey, 63
Hokey Pokey Colors, 44
Hopscotch, Musical, 46
How Can I Compose This?, 146
How D'Ya Do, My Partner, 67
How Many?, 147
How Many?, 154
How Many Got Caught?, 155
Hula Hop, 46
Humming Together, 104

I

I Bought Me a. . . , 115
Improvisation, 114
Indians, 42
Indian Village Messages, 36
Instrument Clue, 173
Instrument Echo, 169
Instrument Match, 173
Instrument Pantomine, 172
Instrument Pitch, 104
Is It the Same?, 84

J

Jim Along Josie, 59
Jumping Jack, 15
Jingle at the Window, 75
Jungle, This Is the, 29

L

Latin American Music, A Learning Center
    for, 191
Leader, I Am the, 20
Let's Pretend, A Music Center for, 188

Line Up, 84
Listening Center, A, 190
Listening Center, A, 196
London Bridge, 56
London Hill, 51
Looby Loo, 53
Long 'n' Short, 39
Loud/Soft Melodies, 81

M

MacDonald, Harl, 83
Magic Hats, 113
Magic Word Song, 111
Making a Song, A Center for, 201
Making a People Melody, 88
Maracas Sound Center, A, 194
Marches, A Learning Center for, 189
Marching Band, 173
Marionette, My, 16
Match Mine, 145
Match My Cylinder, 159
Match the Note Pattern, 91
Matching Note Cards, A Learning Center
    for, 207
Mechanical Man, 43
Melodies With Arrows, 90
Melody Groups, 83
Melody Matching, 88
Melody on a Grid: High, Medium, Low, 93
Melody on a One-Line Staff, 90
Melody on a Two-Line Staff, 90
Missing Persons, 98
Missing Words, 110
Mood Music, 114
Moving On, 36
Mountains, 24
Mountains, Let's Pretend a Trip to the, 24
Muffin Man, 49
Mulberry Bush, 50
Musical Collage, 146
Music Has Feeling, 81
Music Listening, A Story-Book Center for,
    188
Musical Magic Slates, A Music-Writing
    Center with, 205
Music Pattern, A Center for Matching a,
    204
Music Symbols, A Center for Copying, 205
Music Treasure Hunt, 175
Mystery Instrument, 172
Mystic Night, 161

N

Name-Name, 33
Name That Instrument, 174
Name That Sound, 158
Neighborhood, A Walk in My, 28
Nonsense Verse, 101
Notation Center, A, 203
Note Family, The, 80

O

Oats and Beans and Barley Grow, 69
Ocean, This Is the, 29
Old Brass Wagon, 72
Opera Day, 108
Orchestra Around, 173
Orchestra Center, An, 197

P

Pass and Hold, 35
Patriotic Music, A Listening Center for, 189
Paw-Paw Patch, The, 62
Performance Please, 111
Piano Center, 198
Pick the Instrument, 174
Playing Any Instrument, A Center for, 199
Point and Say, 87
Point and Say, 91
Pop! Goes the Weasel, 64
Pound-Sound, 32
Pretend and Pose, 22
Puppets, Learning Center with, 190
Puppet Pets, 107
Puppet Play, 107

R

Read and Play, 88
Reading a Hand Song, 85
Record a Solo, 108
Record Sing-a-Long, A Center for, 201
Remember the Pattern, 38
Resonator Bell Center, 197
Rhyme Dramas, 98
Rhyme Graphing, 100
Rhyme Center, 207
Ring Around the Rosy, 48
Rise, Sally, Rise, 71
Rock and Roll-Over, 17
Round and Round the Village, 73
Rubber Band Center, A, 195

S

Same Pitch Call, 105
Scarves, Fluttering, 17
School, Our, 99
School, The Walk Home From, 161
Secret Messages, 37
Set a Pattern, 91
Set Them Up, 170
Shadow Song, 113
Shapes, 44
Shopping Center, 98
Shopping Center, Let's Pretend a Trip to the, 27
Shoo, Fly!, 60
Sidewalk Steps, 42
Silent Orchestra, 172
Similar Sound, 157
Sing and Go, 110
Sing and Spell, 102
Sing a Song of Sixpence, 52
Sing Me Your Name, 103
Singing a Scale Song, A Center for, 202
Singing a Story, A Center for, 201
Singing Conversation, 102
Singing Game, A Center for a, 203
Singing Puppets, A Center for, 200
Sirens, 103
Skippity Skip, 47
Smooth Move, 41
Softer Sleuth, 109
Sol-Mi Center, 208
Sound-Amplification Center, 194
Sound Boxes, Learning Center for, 192
Sound Categories, 156
Sound-Categorizing Center, 193
Sound Center, A Discovering, 194
Sound-Experiment Center, 195
Sound Groups, 158
Sound Guessing Game, Learning Center, 192
Sound Match, 153
Sound-Matching Center, 193
Sound Signals, 154
Sounds 'N' Squares, 156
Sound Walk, 155
Space, 30
Space Trekking, 30
Staff to Staff, 92
Step Bell Composition, 85
Step My Pattern, 41
Step n' Hold, 39

Stepping Out a Melody, 92
Stop and Go, 35
Storm, 31
Storm, A Walk in the, 31
Swing and Sway, 46

T

Tactile Learning Center for Music, A, 207
Tape the Tap, 157
Taped Peformance, 112
Telephone Talk, 102
Thanksgiving Dinner, 99
Three Bears, A Rhythm Story of, 171
Three Squares, 148
Three-Level Sound, 157
Tight-Rope Walker, The, 16
Timpani, 177
Tiptoe Raindrops, 40
A Tisket, A Tasket, 61
Town, About, 147
Treasure Hunt, 145
Trotting Pony, 42
TV Turn-On, 110

U

Ukulele Center, A, 198

V

Valentine, A, 98
Violin Center, 198
Voices, My Four, 100

W

Walking Casket, The, 176
Walk My Way, 40

Walk on the Stair, A, 86
Waltz, A Listening Center for the, 189
What Did I Do?, 40
What Did I Hear?, 37
What Did You Hear?, 175
What Shape Am I?, 170
Where Am I?, 154
Where's My Family?, 114
Where's the Beat?, 35
Where's the Melody?, 82
Where's the Sound?, 156
Which Am I?, 145
Which is Different?, 83
Which One Am I?, 87
Which One Do You Hear?, 87
Which One Do You Hear?, 145
Which Song Am I?, 108
Which Sound Is Different?, 159
Who Am I?, 147
Who Can?, 43
Who Can Sing It?, 109
Who Has?, 113
Who Is the Composer?, 147
Who Lives at Your House?, 107
Whose Name Is This?, 34
Writing a Composition, A Center for, 206
Writing Directional Melody Patterns, A Center for, 205
Writing Note Words, A Center for, 206
Writing Rhythm Patterns, A Center for, 204
Writing Scales, A Center for, 204

Z

Zoo, Let's Pretend a Trip to the, 26

TOPICAL INDEX

A

Animals, 26, 29, 31, 42, 45, 107, 112
Arrow Cards, 90, 209
Art, 22, 199
Austria, 131
Autoharp, 112, 178, 197
Autumn, 193, 202

B

Ball, 17, 35, 105

Bean Bags, 34, 209
Brass Family, 169, 174, 197

C

Carnival of Animals Suite, 121
Castenets, 179, 180
Chanting, 97, 101
Christmas, 127, 136
Circle, 40, 42, 44, 47-55, 57-61, 63-75, 89
Circle Cards, 174, 209

Circus, 31, 170
City, 30
Clapping, 55, 59, 63, 64, 67
Colors, 44
Composers, 12, 148
    Dukas, 141
    Grieg, 139
    Humperdinck, 128
    Mozart, 131
    Ravel, 133
    Rodgers, 130
    Rossini, 127
    Saint-Saens, 121-126
    Sousa, 143
    Tchaikovsky, 136
Creating Songs, 112-115
Cymbals, 131, 167, 178, 179, 180, 199

D

Danse Macabre, 125
Diatonic Bells, 80, 81, 83, 84, 88, 90, 92,
    167, 177, 178, 179, 180, 197, 199
Drama, 15-22, 24-32, 45, 98, 109, 112, 121-
    143, 188
Drum, 15, 18, 21, 22, 29, 30, 35-38, 41, 42,
    103, 131, 167, 178-180, 195
Dukas, Paul, 141

E

Easter, 45
England, 48-53, 56, 61, 68-69, 73

F

Fantastic Toyshop, 127
Fantasy Stories, 23-32, 45
Farm, 29, 57, 66, 69
Form, 131, 144, 181
Feely Box, 153
Flannelboard, 81, 92
Floorstaff, 81, 82, 84, 88, 92, 210
France, 121, 125, 133, 141

G

Galloping, 39, 41, 42, 45
Germany, 128
Glockenspeil, 177, 178, 199
Grieg, Edvard, 139
Group Singing, 109-115
Guiro, 180

H

Hansel and Gretel, 128
Halloween, 19, 58, 99, 104, 125, 139, 141,
    176, 202
Holt, John, 89
Hopping, 45, 46
Humperdinck, Engelbert, 128
Hula hoops, 46

I

In the Hall of the Mountain King, 139, 181
Indians, 36, 42, 162
Instruments, 163, 167-181, 196-199
Iowa, 64
Ireland, 54
Italy, 127

J

Jumping, 65
Jungle, 29

K

Kentucky, 62

L

Latin America, 191, 194
Learning Centers, 186-208
Listening, 79-84, 188-191

M

Maracas, 167, 178, 180, 191, 194
March of the Siamese Children, 130
Marching, 33, 39, 45, 143, 173, 189
Melody, 79-94
Melody Cards, 85, 87, 88, 91, 210
Messages, 36, 37
Metallophones, 178
Minuet, 131
Mississippi, 71
Montessori, Maria, 79
Mother Goose Suite, 133
Movement, 15-47, 101, 112, 120
Mozart, Wolfgang, 131

N

Name, 33, 34, 103
Norway, 139
Note Discs, 92, 210
Nutcracker Suite, 136, 189

O

Ocean, 29
Oriental, 191
Ostinato, 181
Ozark Mountains, 59

P

Pantomine, 21, 45, 172
Parade, 31
Park, 26
Patriotic, 143, 189
Patterned steps, 38-47
Peer Gynt Suite, 139
Percussion Family, 169, 174, 197
Piaget, Jean, 97
Piano, 15, 23, 24-31, 34, 35, 39-43, 46, 47,
    81-84, 88, 90, 92, 104, 179, 198
Ponies, 42
Puppets, 107, 109, 190, 200

R

Rain, 40
Ravel, Maurice, 133
Reading Melody, 84-88
Recorder, 88-92
Resonator Bells, 37, 83, 101, 104, 167, 170,
    196, 197
Rhythm Ensemble, 178
Rhythm Instruments, 112, 126, 139, 144,
    157, 159
Rodgers, Richard, 130
Rossini, Giovanni, 127
Running, 39, 45, 65
Russia, 136

S

Saint-Saens, Camille, 121, 126
Sand Blocks, 167, 178, 179
Scarves, 17, 41
Set-a-Pattern Cards, 211
Shopping Center, 27
Singing, 97-115, 200-203
Singing Games, 47-75, 109, 203
Skipping, 39, 45, 47, 49, 61, 65, 67, 69, 70,
    71
Sorcerer's Apprentice, 141
Solo Singing, 106-109
Sound Cylinders, 159, 210

Sound Producers, 152
Sounds, 151-163, 192-196
Sousa, John Philip, 143
Springtime, 19, 45, 69
Staff, 90, 91, 92
The Stars and Stripes Forever, 143
Steady Beat, 32-38
Step Bells, 82, 85, 86, 167
Stepping, 39, 41, 45, 82, 92
Sticks, 36, 167, 178, 179, 180
Stories, 23-32, 117, 161, 162, 170, 201
String Family, 169, 197
Swaying, 46
Sweden, 67

T

Tambourines, 167, 178, 179, 180, 199
Tchaikovsky, Peter, 143
Texas, 70
Thanksgiving, 99
Three-Dimensional Music Symbol Cards,
    86, 211
Tiptoe, 40, 45, 65
Tone Blocks, 167, 178
Tone Matching, 101-106
Triangle, 131, 167, 178, 179, 180
Trotting, 39, 42, 45

U

United States, 55, 60, 63, 66, 72, 130, 143

V

Virginia, 65, 74, 75

W

Walking, 39, 40, 43, 45, 82, 86, 155, 161
Waltz, 189
Wood Blocks, 36, 131, 167, 178, 199
Woodwind Family, 169, 174, 197
Writing Melody, 89-94
Writing Music, 203-207

X

Xylophone, 177, 178

Z

Zoo, 26